Academic Tr

MW01517871

"The book *Academic*
any teacher wanting to create a thriving working environment that allows
every student to flourish in their classroom. This book has inspired me to
create a supportive culture in my daily duties while my students and I grow,
learn, and experience authentic learning in my teaching capacity. Dr. Rice's
shared personal journal and inclusion of frameworks such as the Model of
Academic Trust, teacher practice charts, QAR, and Bloom's Taxonomy are
relative to today's educational challenges. He illustrates the fundamental
skills and techniques needed to successfully connect educational leadership
and teachers with students and parents in developing Academic Trust."

~ Gilles Daigle, MEd, BEd Secondary Education

"Academic Trust is a groundbreaking approach to examining the role of
trust in the multifaceted challenges faced by educators and educational
institutions. In addition to extensive research on the science of trust,
Dr. Rice includes situational examples from his years of experience as
an educator and leader. From bullying, to academic achievement, to the
breakdown of interpersonal relationships in the workplace, Academic Trust
is designed as a systems approach to solving problems and building students,
teachers, and schools that exude trust. A highly recommended read for new
and experienced educators, administrators, and educational leaders alike."

~ Richard Jensen , MEd, BEd, BA Secondary Education

"Trust is the foundation of all meaningful and productive relationships. Having
worked alongside Dr. Rice (Tony) he, without a doubt, had the trust of his
students and teachers and he, in turn, trusted those in his charge. That trust was
essential to fostering a culture of change and growth within the school.

"One of the greatest compliments that an educator can receive is that they
'get it.' Those who 'get it,' understand the connection between teaching and
learning, success and failure, and trial and error. Tony most definitely, 'gets
it.' In my role as Vice-Principal, I witnessed, on a daily basis, his dedication
to the iterative process of teaching and learning. In Academic Trust: Closing
the Achievement Gap - A Guide for Teachers, Dr. Rice provides teachers at
every stage of their career the data-driven, research-based evidence behind
'Best Practices' and the tools to implement them into their pedagogy."

~ Michael Pollok, Bed, BA, K-12 Education

"The tools and insights Dr. Rice shares in his book have been instrumental in elevating my teaching and assessment practices. This is required reading for any teacher looking to improve student trust and achievement in the classroom."

~ *Melanie Morter-Erickson, BA, Bed, Elementary Education*

"Over the course of two years, Dr. Rice taught me the basics of exceptional teaching; he was years ahead of his peers on assessment and instruction, and I could always trust him to steer me in the right direction. This book is his Magnum Opus, and I recommend it to any open-minded educator. It is honest, authentic, and applicable, three qualities I look for in any book on education. If you care deeply about your students, then this is the book for you."

~ *Sam Whittleton, BEd Elementary Education*

ACADEMIC TRUST
Closing the Achievement Gap

A Guide for Teachers

DR. TONY RICE

Published in Canada by
Tony Rice Educational Consulting

TONY RICE
EDUCATIONAL CONSULTING

www.DrTonyRice.com

ISBN 978-1-7780350-1-2

Every human endeavour—be it scientific breakthroughs, technological advancements, or advancements in any of the humanities—is rooted in children becoming literate and numerate and learning how to apply these skills to the things that capture their imaginations. This book is dedicated to the many educators that work so very hard at trying to reach every student in their sphere of influence. As a result of your efforts, the world is a better place in so many ways.

Table of Contents

List of Figures and Practice Charts

Figures

Practice Charts

Foreword

STEPHEN COVEY SUGGESTS, "NOTHING IS AS FAST AS THE SPEED OF TRUST. Nothing is as fulfilling as a relationship of trust. Nothing is as inspiring as an offering of trust." With his first venture into the world of authoring a text for colleagues, educator Tony Rice does not shy away from the challenge posed by Covey's words. Instead, he boldly goes where very few educators have ventured and makes the case—the imperative—that all educators must create the conditions for academic trust to flourish. Rice emphatically points out, through twelve strongly connected chapters, that this is the essence of ensuring all students learn and grow, the foundation educators need to close the achievement gap.

Dr. Rice accurately describes this book as "... a good mix of theory and practice all related to building teacher capacity with the goal of developing a classroom culture of academic trust." The book then supports this premise by taking the reader through the various stages of developing this foundation. While not wanting to overwhelm the busy and harried educator, Rice does provide a brief review of the science outlining how our brains sort out trust and distrust experiences, and how neural chemicals play a role in deciding to trust or not to trust. He gives the reader a good review of how our brains operate to develop or inhibit trust and gives insight into the necessary steps to build trust.

Leaders who endeavour to build institutional trust must recognize they are on a journey, a journey that will take time. My work with schools often indicates a three-to-five-year journey (depending on your current baseline) and this book provides a great template to embark on the journey. Rice points out that two elements are essential for developing institutional trust: structural assurance and situational normality. These are complex ideas that Rice makes tangible with great examples and stories from his distinguished career.

The use of diagrams in this book is timely and they really enhance the content of his narrative. Perhaps even more effective than these diagrams are the nine practices that Rice outlines as building capacity opportunities. Charts that accompany each of the practices clearly articulate the potential next steps teams may take on the journey toward building academic trust.

Rice states, "A trusted teacher is perceived to be competent, benevolent, a person of integrity, and empathetic." It is the development of trust that is foundational to ALL students learning and growing. In a conversation with my nine-year-old grandson Liam about what makes his classroom such a positive learning environment, he is quick to point out that his teacher has created a safe space where all students can express their thoughts without fear of being teased. His teacher has established the trust necessary to allow all students to feel confident enough to share interests (he and his friend are exploring quantum physics and the work of Max Planck) and explore learning to the fullest. I have spent a lot of time working with educators on the notion that when students arrive to school they are coming to "our house." It's the only house that we, the educators, have complete control over. Rice validates this approach when he reminds educators that they have the "power to decide what they will do within the walls of their own classroom."

As you work through the book, it will become clear how building academic trust is both essential to, and enhanced by, teacher influence and collective efficacy. Both these elements are in short supply in schools that struggle (driven by a lack of belief in students and colleagues) but thrive in highly functioning schools (where educators believe in each other and in their ability to guarantee learning for all). Rice brings these essential elements home in the final chapters and once again reminds the reader of the power of the team.

The conclusion to the book is a powerful reminder that trust is visceral and fleeting. Our students make rapid decisions about the environments they will spend their school days in, and these decisions impact the learning they will achieve in that content or grade. Rice reminds us that teachers have the capacity and the control over that which matters most in the classroom—their willingness and ability to build relationships with their students that enhance academic trust. I am reminded of the powerful words of Haim Ginott who stated:

> *"I've come to a frightening conclusion that I am the decisive element in the classroom. It's my personal approach that creates the climate. It's my daily mood that makes the weather. As a teacher, I possess a*

tremendous power to make a child's life miserable or joyous. I can be a tool of torture or an instrument of inspiration. I can humiliate or heal. In all situations, it is my response that decides whether a crisis will be escalated or de-escalated, and a child humanized or dehumanized."

I trust you will find this book makes a valuable contribution to your role as an educator and you'll keep it close at hand as you build (or strengthen) your approach to cultivating academic trust and closing the achievement gap.

Tom Hierck
Educational Consultant and Author
Husband, Father, Grandpa, Colleague, Friend and
Relentless Supporter of High Levels of Learning for ALL Students

Introduction

*Teaching is not rocket science. It
is much more complicated.*
Simon Breakspear

Imagine the very first day of your teaching career and hearing from your boss, the principal, "I have made enough mistakes for one day. It is time to go home." Back in 1984, when my professional education journey began, I did not understand the importance and impact of these words when I first heard them. My experience with my first ever administrative team, principal Gary Wesner, and vice-principal Dr. Lloyd Nelson, would go on to shape my professional life beyond any expectations that I could have ever imagined.

My first classroom was across the hallway from Gary's office, and this proximity allowed me to see—and sometimes hear—the best and the worst of the many people who came and went. Gary always tried to influence others with sound reason and judgement, and he never used the authority of his position to overpower them. My classroom location also provided a lot of opportunity to talk shop with Gary. Invariably he would end these conversations with the statement that he had made enough mistakes for one day and that it was time for him to go home. In those first years, everything was new and untried for me. And in the ten years I worked under Gary's administration, I never felt censored when attempting to try something new in my classroom. Not once.

Gary's administrative partner, vice principal Lloyd Nelson was a researcher and a learner. Lloyd earned his PhD when PhDs anywhere, let alone as teachers in public schools, were very rare. However, Lloyd was just Lloyd when it came to being a colleague. He never came across as being better or superior to any of his colleagues. Working with Lloyd led to a lot of classroom experimentation. He could see a willingness in me to try just about anything that might help me to help my students learn. We developed a very fruitful professional relationship—he brought the new ideas, and I tried them in my classroom to see how well they worked. This partnership led to opportunities to share what we worked on in our classrooms with many other school jurisdictions and organizations across the province of Manitoba.

Gary and Lloyd believed that learning was experimental, whether it was a teacher learning about teaching, or a student learning about a school subject. Both administrators clearly communicated that making mistakes meant you were really learning, and that really learning meant that you were making mistakes. Professional capacity building was an iterative experience that improved as less effective teaching practices were rejected and replaced with more effective practices once learned.

At the time, I had no idea that my professional experience with Gary and Lloyd was significantly unique. Their professional beliefs, practices, and approach to teacher capacity building was not common. It was rare then, and unfortunately, I believe it is rare now. As a leadership team, they encouraged, supported, and took advantage of any opportunity to facilitate professional learning by creating a climate of professional trust. There was never any pretense or insinuation that they knew everything and that they were the smartest people in the room, though this may very well have been the case. As a new teacher, I blossomed. I grew in confidence, skill, and capacity, long before capacity building and teacher efficacy were topics of educational discourse.

When Gary and Lloyd moved on from our school, and new leadership arrived, it became very clear to me how influential and important school leadership was. The cohesive team, with the exceptional leadership that I had worked with for years, very quickly lost its way. The new school leadership were good people with good intentions, but their skill set did not include the skills necessary to maintain and propagate the culture of professional trust and collaboration that had previously prevailed. As a result, the well-developed cultural norms that supported professional trust did not survive. Protectionism and isolationism became the new norm. Why? Because central to the creation of professional trust is the foundation of relational trust. School leadership needs to be seen as competent, interpersonally respectful, having regard for others, and as persons of integrity by those who are assigned to work with them (Robinson, 2011). Failure to meet these requirements will lead to the development of a dysfunctional school culture to one degree or another. With little relational trust, the school culture of iterative, collaborative, professional learning could not survive. The school I had learned to love and work in became a place where I became very uncomfortable. This singular experience led me to consider the importance of school leadership and how it contributes to an environment that supports collaborative team development.

While this aspect of schools and districts is important for teachers to grasp and understand, *Academic Trust: Closing the Achievement Gap* will provide a model of *academic trust* to guide teachers in their professional career. The purpose is to first introduce teachers to the concept of academic trust and then delineate how this new concept is grounded in contemporary interpersonal and institutional trust research, explain the required strategies and approaches to create this supportive culture, and then conclude with how it can be developed in each classroom with every student. Every teacher, independent of school and district systems, can successfully create a classroom culture that supports an environment of academic trust. While I was fortuitously placed in the right school at the right time, not many get to experience the high level of professional collaborative culture that I did when beginning my career. There may be pockets of it here and there in many school buildings and between some teachers and their students, but to have it permeate an entire school is rare. For those who create and experience this kind of work environment—hats off to all of you.

Together, Gary and Lloyd exemplified leadership. Their trust in their team translated into trusting relationships throughout the school, including teacher trust of students, and their attempt to create a trusting environment helped every student to flourish. After much consideration and time, this work is a product of that time and place and its people. Anyone who digs into this book will come away better for having devoted the energy to it. There is a good mix of theory and practice all related to building teacher capacity with the goal of developing a classroom culture of academic trust.

1

Trust—The Bigger Picture

Trust is the glue of life. It's the most essential ingredient in effective communication. It's the foundational principle that holds all relationships.
Stephen R. Covey

UNDERSTANDING TRUST IS A PROFITABLE ENDEAVOUR FOR ALL EDUCATORS simply because they are in the trust business. Without a high level of trust, teaching and learning will not take place. Unfortunately, trust in public education is currently being undermined by forces such as top-down decision making and high-stakes external testing, creating pockets of systemic distrust that will take a long time to recover from.

Contemporary trust research has much to offer the field of public education. Therefore, the first three chapters of this book will offer a brief review of the science outlining how our brains sort out trust and distrust experiences, and how neural chemicals play a role in deciding to trust or not to trust. Determinants of institutional and interpersonal trust, and how these two types of trust are essential for success in the educational arena, is explored. A model of academic trust is introduced, and its components are briefly explained. The reader will begin to understand just how complex the teaching process is and how it is especially complicated by trust issues.

Academic Trust: A Conceptual Framework

Academic trust is a new construct and at the beginning stages of being clearly defined. As illustrated in Figure 1, the teacher and the student bring to the learning relationship their current attitudes related to institutional and interpersonal trust. Much of this is subconscious and dynamic in its development. Individual personal experience continues to impact these two types of trust propensities. There are two components of academic trust that connect the student learner and the teacher to permit optimum teaching and learning to occur. Firstly, academic trust requires that the student learner is willing to be vulnerable and accept the social, intellectual, and emotional risks of revealing to the teacher that they do not understand what it is that the teacher is trying to teach, and they are willing to do so in the presence of other learners, their classmates. Secondly, it requires that the teacher has created a learning environment that allows the learner to feel sufficiently confident socially, intellectually, and emotionally so that they would not see instructional correction as an attack on their competency as a learner. The learner can openly discuss "not knowing" with the teacher, in front of peers, with the intent of being able to know the intended learning target. The learner can engage in learning with confidence. Academic trust is a two-way street influenced by students and teachers.

Figure 1
Academic Trust Conceptual Framework

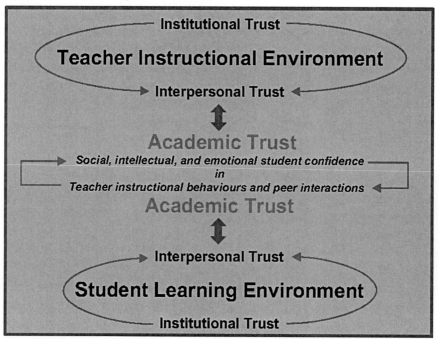

In essence, high academic trust exists when the learning environment has become so student–centred and focused on the learning that there exists a collective student group–efficacy, wherein every student feels sufficient confidence that the learning environment is void of any negative influences surrounding their individual capacity to learn. In this environment, it is acceptable to make mistakes and to not know.

Like trust, academic trust is not an all or nothing occurrence. Academic trust manifests itself on a continuum, from little or no trust, to strong or high trust. Context does matter. One student may have high academic trust that includes a small group of peers and the teacher, but low academic trust when the entire class is included. Another student can feel high levels of academic trust regardless of who is in the classroom because of how they perceive themselves in relation to the teacher and their peers. This student may have high levels of social, intellectual, and emotional confidence and easily interact with everyone without fear of judgement, particularly from their peers.

The Science of Trust

Randy Borum in *The Science of Interpersonal Trust* (2010) summarizes the trust research of Stephen Porges (2001, 2003, & 2007). Borum sets forth, first and foremost, that an understanding of trust is essential for improving the performance of individuals and organizations, and secondly, that deception and trust are not opposing concepts but coexist simultaneously. These two ideas, as they relate to education today are examined. Public school systems are compelled to improve. At the heart of this compulsion is the trust-distrust dynamic. Governments, the public, and the media wrestle with whether society is getting the best outcomes for the money spent, and their reactions have resulted in an inordinate amount of scrutiny, implicitly embracing the distrust side of the equation. Learning what trust research has to offer school systems is fundamental to government and politics, the public, and the media leaning more in the direction of trusting those who work in the school system, particularly those who teach in it. So, what does science contribute to the trust-distrust discussion?

Antecedents of Interpersonal Trust

Does trust start from a neutral, positive, or negative baseline? The neutral or zero-baseline theory is the traditional position (Blau, 1964; Rempel et al., 1985). What is a normal or routine school circumstance? We all come to our schools with a trust starting point determined by our own school experience, cultural factors, expectations for our children, and current relationships with those working in schools. In routine circumstances we typically choose to suspend belief that the other person is untrustworthy, and we choose to trust (Jones & George,1998). Other factors include our own trust propensity, which is determined by our temperament, personality characteristics, and even genotype factors (McKnight et al., 1998; Rotter, 1980; Rotter & Stein, 1971). Those who work at the school often influence the trust position of those who interact with them solely on the reputation that is prevalent within the community about them, be it positive or negative.

Regardless of the trustor's starting point, be it neutral, negative, or positive, what factors influence their decision to trust the trustee? The first is the perceived ability of a person to be trusted by the trustor. Does the trustor see the trustee as someone that is competent, predictable, and consistent? A person working in a school doesn't have to be in a school community long before students share their perceptions of their teacher's ability with family and friends. Students quickly decide how capable a teacher is. Parents then form opinions from shared information from their children and others connected to the school community. A second factor is perceived levels of benevolence. Does the student see the teacher as a person of goodwill? Being perceived as benevolent by students is an essential character trait for someone working with children. A third factor is integrity. Do teachers do what they say they will do and what they committed to do? Are teachers fair, accurate, and honest in their dealings with other colleagues, parents, and most importantly students? The greater the degree to which a teacher is perceived as a person of ability, benevolence, and integrity, the greater the degree of trustworthiness granted to that teacher.

Jason Colquitt and his colleagues (2007) found that the three primary determinants of trust—ability, benevolence, and integrity—coupled with the disposition to trust and the emotional response to trust are the major determinants of trust. Ability, benevolence, and integrity significantly determine affective commitment. To tie these components together in terms of their importance:

> Affective commitment is one's desire to be part of a collective or group because of social and emotional bonds, not just for the tangible incentives (Shore, et al., 2006). The trustworthiness triad was so robust that it predicted trust behaviors and bonds even with different trust measures, with a wide range of trustees, and in different kinds of relationships. (Borum, p. 15)

For teachers, the implications of these major determinants of trust and their impact on healthy relationships in a school system cannot be overstated.

Thinking and Feeling Trust

To be perceived as trustworthy permits others to think and feel that you can be trusted—two separate but complementary processes. To be able to think that you can trust someone, there must be enough information to deliberate upon, to weigh options, and to come to a decision to trust or not to trust. Prior experience, including how well you know a person, their credentials and reputation, and the level of expectation attached to the task are all part of the cognitive process of determining the level of trust granted to someone. Depending upon the information considered, this cognitive deliberation can shift trust from a neutral to a positive or negative expectation. This is called cognitive-based trust (McAllister, 1995).

In personnel interviews and in consideration of offering a particular teaching position, how those who are responsible for the interview feel about a candidate strongly influences their decision, in addition to what they think. Do those who conduct the interview feel they connect with the person being interviewed? Do they feel the candidate is on the same page, sharing the same beliefs, goals, and interests? Is the candidate seen as someone that will fit into and contribute to the existing school team and culture? If those involved in the interview make an emotional bond with the candidate and check all the cognitive boxes, the candidate will do better. This is an example of affective-based trust (McAllister, 1995).

It can be argued that cognitive and affective trust, in addition to being different kinds of trust, mark different stages of trust (Lewicki & Bunker, 1996). When individuals initially meet and have little information about each other to base decisions on, or have no emotional connection to each other, cognitive trust weighs the benefits of behaving in a trustworthy manner versus the costs of betrayal. In short-term relationship circumstances, where little risk is required and betrayal opportunities unlikely, nothing more may be required than limited cognitive trust. Rousseau et al. (1998) suggest that cognitive trust takes a back seat to affective trust when time spent together permits relationships to deepen. Affective trust drives knowledge and understanding of each other, perceived stability and behaviour over time, shared experiences, and proximity. Past cooperative ventures allow emotional bonds and connections to be made that seal trust. This shift from cognitive to affective trust may involve a "transformation of motivation" (Kelly, 1984) from individual self-interest to interest in group outcomes and success. Schools and school systems need to consider the dynamic of how to build and deepen professional learning communities when attempting to set and achieve goals where high-risk trust and vulnerability play a role and individual commitment is required. Leadership decisions that significantly impact teachers need to be considered in light of the impact on both cognitive and affective trust. When leadership decisions impact subordinates negatively, trust is seriously damaged, impacting the output of the whole system. A litmus test for leadership impact is to determine how everyone is feeling. Trust coherence will leave most feeling positive. On the other hand, feelings of frustration and confusion among subordinates who do not see the wisdom of system decisions and direction are sure signs of internal system distrust. Those who must carry out institutional goals and direction can ensure buy-in through fostering an environment of interpersonal and institutional trust.

2

Deciding to Trust— Heuristics and the Brain

The brain is the most complex, challenging scientific
puzzle we have ever tried to decode.
Paul Allen, Co-Founder
of Microsoft

HISTORICALLY, TRUST DECISIONS WERE A RATIONAL PROCESS OF WEIGHING "What's in it for me?" versus "What is it going to cost me?" as a calculation. While this calculation may be a part of the process of deciding to trust or not to trust, it does not fully add up. A clear, systematic, predictable pattern is not discernible. The current thinking is that heuristics—mental shortcuts—are used to decide trust issues simply because the complexity of the social context we all exist in is much too intricate for our brains to come to terms with quickly and easily. These rules-of-thumb do not always result in the best decisions, but they are often good enough. Borum (2010) explains three cognitive processes that are used to determine trust decisions that are good enough.

The first is that "our limited brains, in order to function efficiently, attempt to simplify our complex world" (p. 26). Stereotypes, prejudices, and biases are implicitly used to render trust decisions when appearance, gender, and race are considered. We must clearly understand that not all stereotypes, prejudices, and biases are negative. All of us use these shortcuts, all the time, to simplify the complexity of our context. Experiments demonstrate that when a picture of a person deemed untrustworthy is viewed, the amygdala—the fear centre of the brain—is activated. It has also been demonstrated that when given more time to consider more information that our decisions do not get better, they get worse. This simplification process serves most of us well, most of the time.

The second cognitive trend is that "Human brains are wired to make decisions about options and value based on comparisons, not in absolute terms." When given two options that are identical in terms of outcomes, how the options are framed is significant. The following experiment illustrates this notion:

A group of people are given a scenario in which 600 people are in peril, and they must decide between two courses of action. Half are given the first frame: "Option A will save 200." The other half are given the second frame: "Option B will allow 400 people to die." The phrasing of the first frame emphasizes the number of lives saved, while the second frame emphasizes the number of deaths. The actual probabilities are identical, but more people choose Option A, the first frame, than its alternative (Kühberger, 1995; Tversky & Kahneman, 1981). A team of researchers (De Martino, et al., 2006) used this task in an fMRI study and found each of the two frames produced different patterns of activation in the amygdala ... and correlated strongly with the chosen course of action, suggesting emotions were responsible for the framing effect. Interestingly, however, task-related activity in the brain's higher-level thinking and reasoning areas (the prefrontal cortex) mitigated susceptibility to the framing effect. (p. 28)

Accordingly, how we frame issues is as important as the issue when it comes to attempting to gain trust.

The final cognitive trend is, "Our expectations affect our judgments and outcomes." Can you predict what one study showed if you were in significant pain and you had a choice between a painkiller that is worth a dime or one that is worth $2.50? The implicit notion is that "you get what you pay for" because quality costs more. When given the $2.50 placebo, people reported more pain relief than with the dime painkiller. Clearly, we see what we expect to see because of confirmation bias. The implications for education systems and those working in them are powerful. "Indeed, prior studies have found that an untrustworthy reputation evokes feelings of distrust (Deutsch, 1960; Lewicki & Bunker, 1995, 1996)" (Borum, p. 28). Confirmatory bias can also be positive. As we interact with people over time, we can come to appreciate what they are able to contribute to the group.

Stereotypes, prejudices, biases, comparisons, framing a set of circumstances, and confirmation bias all play into our decisions to trust, helping us to simplify our complex world. What are the professional and practical implications for these cognitive processes that we are unaware of, and how do these sub-conscious beliefs and impulses impact attempts to build a trusting teaching and learning environment?

Looking at the Brain

There are two devices used for measuring brain activity to help determine brain function. The first is the use of EEG or electroencephalography. This device can measure neural firings as they occur in real time in the brain. The second is fMRI, or functional magnetic resonance imaging. This device can measure the ratio of oxygenated to deoxygenated hemoglobin blood flow in the brain and the location of that blood flow. Together these two devices can help identify what signal the brain is picking up on, and what part of the brain is responding to the signal. Given that these two tools are what is available to study trust as it relates to the brain and how and where the brain responds, it is clear that this work is far from conclusive and much more work needs to be done in terms of research design, technical measurement, and coming to firm conclusions. That said, partial insight into the inner workings of the brain is better than no insight at all.

Neuroscience and brain imaging have allowed researchers to examine the brain as it responds to social dilemma games. During these games, the brain responds quite differently to characters considered to be cooperators and defectors. Becoming involved with defectors activates the amygdala, the brain's fear centre. The brain also responds differently between intentional coopera-tors and non-intentional cooperators, suggesting that intention is relevant to the brain, though the outcomes are identical. Thus, doing the right things for the right reasons or the right things for the wrong reasons is distinguishably different. Borum writes that the nature of those differences in brain activation suggests "subjects were not simply learning which faces were associated with reward. They were learning whom to trust" (Frith & Frith, 2006, p. 38).

In another game, participants were paired with a character that was either portrayed as being neutral, praiseworthy, or morally suspect. The counterpart partners played with a 50% cooperation/reinforcement schedule (Borum, p. 30). The experiment found that:

> Significant activation of the striatum was only observed when
> participants thought they were playing with the morally "neutral"

partner, not when playing the morally "good" partner. In fact, as people played the game through multiple iterations—even though they only achieved "cooperation" half the time—participants persistently made more risky choices when they thought the partner had a good moral reputation. Thus, prior expectations about an individual drove their judgments and, in some cases, inhibited their ability to learn from their experiences (Delgado, Frank, & Phelps, 2005).

These experimental games demonstrate that "Confirmatory biases and reputation-based expectations ... can sometimes override interpersonal experiential learning" (Borum, p. 30). This could be positive or negative depending on the position of the bias and expectations. The result in a school system is that some teachers, students, or parents will not receive a fair judgement regardless of their real intent and motives. This is a real concern. Being aware of the roles of stereotyping, framing, and confirmation bias is a good place to begin to examine the issue of fairness and trust.

Automatic and Controlled Brain Processing Systems

The brain has two distinct systems for processing information—the automatic and the controlled. The automatic system is driven by emotion and intuition, while the controlled system is driven by logic and reason. The automatic system is slow, while the controlled system is fast. The automatic system is less affected by cognitive load, while the controlled system is more affected when cognitively loaded. The automatic system is sensitive to subliminal influences, while the controlled system is not. The automatic system is insensitive to nuances and exceptions to the rule, while the controlled system is sensitive to these influences. Finally, the automatic system is a slow learner, while the controlled system is a fast learner. This dual processor model is impacted by a range of hormones, neurochemicals, and perceptual factors, and they work together taking advantage of each other's strengths and weaknesses as each relates to specific tasks and circumstances.

New social introductions and novel situations are more emotionally driven; however, the controlled system will influence our confirmation biases and emotional impulses so that logic and reason are also included in the new interactions. As these novel situations become more common, we learn to function with less emotion and more control, allowing us to feel more comfortable in these novel situations. Borum explains, "The rational-emotional balance is a critical component in regulating our social behavior—likely so with trust as well" (p. 31). New teachers attending their first parent-teacher interviews experience this balancing act. Borum quotes Lewis and Weigert (1985) explaining, "trusting behavior may be motivated primarily by strong positive affect for the object of trust or by 'good rational reasons' why the object of trust merits trust, or, more usually, some combination of both. Trust in everyday life is a mix of feeling and rational thinking." Interpersonal social interactions resource unique brain functions.

How do we make decisions about trust in social contexts? Contemporary research (Jackson et al., 2006; Morrison et al., 2007) suggests strongly that when a social interaction begins between two or more parties, each participant's brain begins to function in a similar manner as each person attempts to understand the emotional and mental state of the other, while accessing the same neural pathways. Borum (2010) asserts that "At the most fundamental, biological level, there is accumulating evidence that our own neural systems detect and mimic what we observe in others. A recently popular hypothesis is that this is the effect of a mirror neuron system (Rizzolatti & Craighero, 2004)."

This mirroring process that takes place in social interactions is more than just reflexive; it is intentional, and the depth of neural activity is impacted by the degree of eye contact between those involved in the social interaction (Kilner et al., 2006). Several brain locations that have been activated have been identified as mirror neurons. (Iacoboni & Daprettto, 2006; Rizzolatti & Craighero, 2004). As trustor and trustee interact, their brains are activated as they strive to determine the amount of trust that will result between them. Borum (2010) explains that "Empathic processes are a key part of how people assess others' intentions. These are the processes that allow us to understand and even share others' emotional and feeling states (De Vignemont & Singer, 2006)" (p. 33). Borum adds, "when we empathize, we are aware that our reactions and feeling states are prompted by someone else's reactions and experiences (Lamm, Porges, Caicoppo & Decety, 2008). We are—with awareness—viewing a situation from another person's perspective." Accordingly, the level of empathy experienced by the participants is directly related to the strength of the emotional bond and the intensity of the interaction being experienced.

In addition to accessing empathetic processes, mentalizing, "the very conscious and deliberate processes we use to infer or predict what others are thinking and feeling" (Frith & Singer, 2008), is also engaged in determining trust in social situations. What we know about this process comes from research participants reacting to being shown pictures and stories of people and being asked what the people in the pictures might be thinking and feeling. Consistently, these studies show the parts of the brain that are used for evaluating others and determining altruism and ethical and moral decision making, as well as the area that helps us to decide the meaning of both our feelings and the current experience (Frith & Frith, 2003; Saxe et al., 2004). When experiments involve participants playing against people and against computers, these areas of the brain are activated only when people are involved and not the computer (McCabe et al., 2001; Rilling et al., 2004).

EEG and fMRI are helping us to observe how the brain functions as it strives to interpret situations that require us to trust and be trusted. While these are beginning steps, they offer us much to consider.

Neurochemicals and Behaviour

The brain is basically composed primarily of gray matter, neurons, and chemicals. Oxytocin, vasopressin, and dopamine are three chemicals that the brain uses on a regular basis and are related to numerous physiological and psychological processes, one of those being trust.

Oxytocin

Oxytocin (OT) has been referred to as the love hormone (September, 2017, medicalnewstoday) because it is connected to bonding behaviours, the creation of group memories, social recognition, positive social behaviours, relaxation, trust, psychological stability, and it downregulates stress responses, including anxiety (Neumann, 2007). Other research demonstrates that when OT was administered to participants in research game situations, reciprocity and generosity increased, even when risk-taking itself did not change, suggesting OT's effects are very specific and sensitive to the social context (Kosfeld et al., 2005). When OT was administered to participants who were being tested on their ability to infer another's internal state, they were able to do so with greater accuracy (Domes et al., 2007). Deciding who to trust, with what, to what degree, and under what conditions is an essential component of navigating social situations, and OT seems to be an active ingredient in helping us to do so. The finding above led to a follow-up study requiring participants to infer what the person in a picture is thinking and feeling, when shown only the eyes and the area around the eyes. The treatment group performed significantly better, and more so with the more complex inferences (Domes et al., 2007). Within these studies, a small sub-group, approximately 2%, did not respond to OT treatments like the other participants. This group demonstrated callus, detached, unemotional disregard for others and were identified as possible psychopaths by some.

OT is an important hormone that deserves further study. Currently, this neurochemical appears to play a positive role in helping most of us to decide when it is appropriate and not appropriate to trust.

Vasopressin

Vasopressin (VP) is another hormone that is very similar to OT. Its impact seems to be different between men and women. Borum reports (2010) that, "it has also been associated with male-typical social behaviors, including aggression, pair bonding, scent marking, and courtship" (Heinrichs et al., 2009). Centrally active VP seems generally to be associated with increased vigilance, anxiety, arousal, and activation. Interestingly, increases in OT usually suppress VP. Recent research indicates that there is an OT – VP pathway and that these two hormones work together (Carter, 2017). Both hormones interact to mitigate and influence our perceptions of fear and safety. VP is implicated in our attempts to defend self and family. Both hormones interacting is likely required for sexual and paternal behaviour, and pair bonding. In this pathway, OT is more likely responsible for how we adapt to high levels of social engagement, our sense of safety within family or familiar social groups, our emotional regulation, and higher levels of rational cognition, attachment and bonding, and protection (Carter, 2017). VP influences circadian rhythms, impacts sleep disturbances, elevations in blood pressure, and is connected to posttraumatic stress disorders and male emotional dysregulation and aggression (Carter, 2017). VP also needs further study, particularly in how it interacts with OT and how together they impact our behaviours related to interpersonal trust. It appears that VP plays a role in helping to warn us that the context we are in is possibly a dangerous one and that we need to pay attention. Teachers need to trust these messages and act accordingly.

Dopamine

Dopamine, active in several parts of the brain, is another important neuro-chemical connected primarily to the brain's reward system. It assists us in social situations to understand incoming information to determine the level of reward, pleasure, social disturbances and fear, and reward-based learning opportunities. Thus, the interplay between our perceptions of fear, threat, and reward are physiologically impacted by the levels of dopamine in our brain as we decide when to trust, whom to trust, and under what circumstances to trust. Our brain, at both conscious and unconscious levels, assesses social situations and helps us to navigate social norms and expectations. It helps us see events from other perspectives, read facial expressions and body language, sort out ambiguity and mixed signals, and then determine the level of intrapersonal trust required for the specific situation, and it assists in control of our emotional and cognitive input to determine an appropriate response. Dopamine is connected to our movement and speech, thus influencing our body language and conversation as we interact in social groups. With regard to movement, lack of dopamine is connected to Parkinson's, a movement disease.

Dopamine is also the reward chemical that makes us feel good, thus participating in repetitive behaviours to continue to feel the reward of dopamine is connected to addiction behaviours. Eating too much because we enjoy the food can lead to overeating, but dopamine doesn't care about that. The reward—chasing the feeling of enjoying good-tasting food—is the goal. Using heroin, nicotine, and cocaine creates a huge spike in dopamine release, creating the high from the drug, leading to addiction and negative life consequences. Dopamine is a two-edged sword that is necessary for developing healthy personal behaviours in socially dynamic environments in school. Yet school environments will continue to deal with the negative aspects of dopamine addictive behaviours displayed by students and their parents and have to realize that these negative behaviours are not repaired or mitigated with a stern talking to. Typical school approaches are often counter-productive. Identifying addictive behaviours in students, and then dealing with them according to best practice, requires resources above and beyond what is typically available in most schools.

We know that our brains are physiologically set up to search after reward and to avoid threats to self. Our survival depends upon these processes. The three neurochemicals—oxytocin, vasopressin and dopamine—are just a small sample of those that are actively influencing the decisions we make each day to survive and hopefully flourish. No two lives are identical. While on the surface, some lives appear to be better—and in some cases, much better—than others, each are subject to how the person's brain functions and how they are able to perceive the world that they live in. One of the most gifted, intelligent, funny, personable, students I have ever taught, who appeared to have everything going for him in his teenage years, chose to end his life in his early twenties with the onset of schizophrenia. Sadly, brain neurochemistry determined his outcome despite all that he appeared to have going for him. In schools all over the world, brain neurochemistry is, in large part, impacting how well our young people are doing or not doing, and not enough attention is paid to this fact. Because behaviour is complicated, teaching is complicated.

Motivation and learning research are far ahead of the outdated industrial school systems that currently operate in most parts of the world. Furthermore, the current reward-failure techniques that systematically disengage so many students need serious reconsideration because of new understandings about what motivates students and how they actually learn. Chasing marks is not the same as learning and can be a very poor substitute for learning. Pope (2001) demonstrated that very successful students, as seen by their peers, their teachers and by their marks, manipulated, cheated, and lied to achieve the marks they had. Many students figure out at an early age that school has been organized to rank and sort, and those motivated by marks quickly learn how to get them. Incidentally, most students are not motivated by marks, so why do we continue to use them in the manner that we do? Brain chemistry and youth behaviour is complex and there is certainly more to be learned about these important things, particularly as they relate to the trust relationship.

A Note about Psychopathy

A lot of resources are spent on ensuring safe and welcoming school environments. A universal focus for schools is anti-bullying. A Google search reveals 325,000,000 websites, in 0.43 seconds, dedicated to bullying and how to deal with it. My experience in schools has demonstrated that bullying, and the possible neurochemical brain connection that may underlie some of the behaviours identified as such, is simply not addressed in any meaningful way. Making the distinction between youth that are behaving badly as a behaviour issue, versus youth who are fundamentally maladaptive, are different issues and demand different approaches.

Psychopaths have serious deficits in identifying social cues, producing socially appropriate responses or reactions, and regulating emotional reactions and behavioural responses (Phillips et al., 2003a; 2003b). Further, they have difficulty understanding others' facial expressions and use of language, in recognizing sadness and fear in others, and are unable to use inhibitory controls and executive function (Gao & Raine, 2009). Executive function controls high-level reasoning, impulsive actions and influences social sensitivity, social awareness, and empathy (Herba et al., 2007).

Borum (2010) shares that the brains of people who exhibit persistent antisocial and interpersonally transgressive behaviour and who show little empathy or emotional regard for others have brains that are structurally different than the brains of normal controls (Raine, 2008). These structural differences tend to be most pronounced in areas of the brain associated with processing of social/emotional information and regulatory functions, which also happens to be the areas integral to trust-related processes. The centres for regulating behaviour and emotion and interpreting fear tend to be smaller and have fewer neurons, while the areas that regulate conditioning and learning are asymmetrical. The area of the brain connected to healthy interpersonal emotional responsiveness and feelings of social attachment and remorse are also thinner and result in diminished responses by these individuals.

In addition to brain structural differences, other research suggests genetics may play a role. Of the 3,200,000,000 genes we all have, 3,000,000 are different. This 0.1% accounts for all our individual differences. Genome research has demonstrated that very small changes in gene sequencing can have a substantial impact on these individual differences. One gene in 3,200,000,000 connected to OT receptors is likely responsible for the social attachment deficit in people with autism spectrum disorder. Another example of the impact of gene change is that the deletion of about twenty-five genes is responsible for the disproportionate trusting behaviours of those who have William's Syndrome. While no DNA gene trust centre has yet been identified, to suggest that there might be one is not unreasonable. It is likely that as research continues with the human genome, there will be more connections made between disease and behaviour concerns as a result of gene variation.

Despite all attempts that teachers make to find a way to connect some children to positive interpersonal trusting relationships and positive behaviour patterns, sometimes it doesn't happen because the child just cannot do it.

There is much we do not know about the brain, its neurochemistry, DNA influences, and brain malfunction, but sometimes the traditional approaches to school discipline cannot help some students.

In rare circumstances, student maladaptive behaviours are beyond the scope of regular school support. Normally functioning brains are strongly influenced by the automatic and controlled brain processes and OT helps to regulate these processes. When students do not respond to the strongest intervention levels offered by most schools, it is time to consider that something more is going on than a student misbehaving. While it may be uncomfortable, it is a hard reality that socio and psychopaths are alive and well and attending school in their youth. Recognizing this fact and dealing with it in a proactive manner is more helpful than pretending that these students are not in our schools. Some students require more complex interventions if any positive impact is to be gained. We do know that the brain, its neurochemicals, genetics, and brain malfunctioning all play a significant role in determining behaviour, and the more we understand these influences, the better it will be for all involved when it comes to teaching and student learning.

3

Institutional Trust and the Academic Trust Model

Trust is the highest form of human motivation.
Stephen Covey

How important is institutional trust? A quick Google search will reveal how many of the globe's most important companies, organizations, and institutions—indeed, our entire economic sector—strive to be known as the most trusted in their field. This clearly demonstrates the massive global interest and importance ascribed to institutional trust. With all this interest generated by our largest economic institutions, this begs the questions, what is institutional trust, why all the attention, and what can educational institutions learn from this?

Two factors define institutional trust: structural assurance and situational normality (McKnight et al., 1998). Structural assurance is how one perceives the set of guarantees, safety nets, and other structures that are in place to permit confidence to exist in what is expected will be delivered, thus allowing trust to exist. Situational normality is the belief that everything is unfolding as it should, in its customary, normally expected manner. An example is going to a bank to withdraw cash by inserting a bank card into the ATM and having the cash delivered as expected. Institutional trust requires banks to keep your money safe, make it available to you, that the technology will deliver it as requested, and that you can obtain it in the customary manner.

The emotional trust connection of interpersonal trust relationships is replaced with cognitive trust as we navigate the anonymity of larger, complex, structured systems. Many of our day-to-day business transactions take place with individuals we do not know and as a result cannot emotionally trust. However, because these individuals represent trusted institutions, we carry out the business of purchasing houses, automobiles, and securing the commodities of life, and making a living with a fairly high level of trust. We do this because we know that there are specific safeguards in place that we count on, such as legal contracts, new home warranties, and new purchase return policies. Structural assurances and situational normalities allow us to feel protected.

Trust is always connected to risk. If I decide to trust, what happens if I am wrong? Will I be able to bear the cost of being wrong? When it comes to interpersonal trust, the cost of being wrong is limited to dealing with just one other party. Will they or won't they fulfill my expectation of trust? Institutional trust has many more layers, thus more complexity. Other structural and situational circumstances may lead to increased suspicion and lack of trust. Consider institutional trust from the perspective of different population groups dealing with the institution of government. Will their trust baseline start at neutral, positive, or negative? Consider four different cohorts: an English European natural born Canadian cohort, a recent white Mexican Mennonite Canadian cohort, a Plains Cree Canadian cohort, and a Somalian Canadian immigrant cohort. Would the trust baseline for each of these cohorts be the same? Let's add age groups to these cohorts as another filter. Consider a 15-year-old cohort, a 35-year-old cohort, and a 65-year-old cohort and consider the trust baseline for each of these cohorts and how they may be different. It is likely that there would be differences between and possibly within these different cohorts based upon their place of birth, ethnic background, and age.

Other institutional trust filters that shape trust propensity are socioeconomic status, gender, political ideology, and personal and group governmental interactions, just to name a few. These multiple layers illustrate institutional trust complexity, and understanding these multiple layers is extremely important in the light of working with school populations. To emphasize, consider three different schools and the implications for how each population may perceive institutional trust and how this may impact the work of the school. The first school is in a large, multi-ethnic, inner-city location, where the majority population is overwhelmingly people of colour. The second school is in a small, rural, traditional agricultural community where the population is primarily white. The third school is in a northern reserve community where the population is primarily Indigenous. Now consider that the teaching population in each of these schools is predominantly white. What kinds of institutional trust issues do each of these different community cultural conditions create? Each school, and their respective communities, will negotiate institutional trust differently, taking into consideration the local culture and norms and differences. When it comes to institutional trust, one size does not fit all.

Despite the complex layers of institutional trust, it is achievable on a large scale. As Lewis and Weigert (1985) explain "System trust is indispensable for the effective functioning of the 'symbolic media of exchange' such as money and political power. Without public trust and confidence in the reliability, effectiveness, and legitimacy of money, laws, and other cultural symbols, modern social institutions would soon disintegrate (see Parsons, c, d)" (p. 974). For institutional trust to break down to this degree, some catastrophic societal event must take place including such forces as war, economic breakdown, or large scale politically oppressive actions. The current impact of the COVID-19 pandemic, the social "Me Too" and "Black Lives Matter" movements, and the 2020 USA election clearly illustrate the fragility of institutional trust and the roles of structural assurance and situational normality. In addition, there have been many forces, be they political conflict and war, environmental disaster, or economic upheaval that have challenged structural assurance and situational normality, impacting institutional trust stability around the globe.

A Model of Academic Trust

While others have circumlocuted the concept of academic trust, it has never been named. For example, Shelley Harwayne (1999) clearly describes its essence when she shared this insight:

> I learned a long time ago that it doesn't matter what curriculum decisions we make, what instructional strategies we try, or what assessment tools we select, if students and teachers don't care about each other. It doesn't matter how brilliant our mini lessons are or how clever our conferences are if children make fun of each other's handwriting, dialect, or choice of topic. These things don't matter at all if the really important stuff isn't in place. Children will not share significant stories, take risks as spellers, or accept new challenges if the classroom is not secure or supportive (p. 104) as quoted in (Hierck, Coleman & Weber, 2011, pp. 39-40).

So, what is in a name? Naming something gives it life, an identity, and power, and separates it from all other named things. Providing this newly named concept with its own meaning and purpose allows this new concept to be autonomous and then clearly understood. And because it is clearly understood, it is therefore knowable and thus teachable. Thus, the enhancement of academic trust is a force that unleashes innate childhood curiosity and a safer learning environment, creating a greater willingness to learn. Learning is a sacred opportunity meant to be experienced by every child that has ever stepped foot inside a classroom.

Figure 2 shows a model of academic trust. This model outlines the elements that regulate the creation of a learning environment that supports high academic trust.

Figure 2
Academic Trust Model

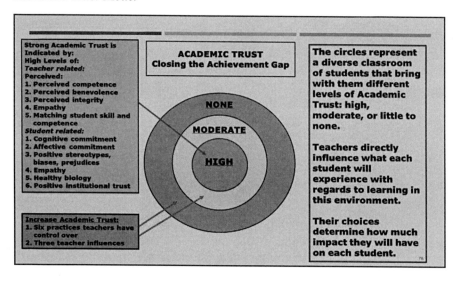

Several things must be in place for high levels of academic trust to flourish. As outlined in the top left box, students must perceive the teacher as a competent instructor, a person of benevolence and integrity, as empathetic and able to meet each student where they are at with regard to matching their skill set with the appropriate level of academic challenge. The student is more likely to commit cognitively and affectively to a trusting learning relationship with a teacher they perceive as having these qualities. In addition, students bring to the instructional environment their own stereotypes, prejudices, biases, framing, confirmation bias, their own sense of empathy, their biological state, and their view of institutional trust. Teachers must be able to navigate the students' sense of trust in order to build on it. On the surface, the standard implied by the model may appear to be impossible to measure up to, and we know that many students do not come to our classrooms as prepared and ready as we would like them to be. We also know that the longer a student is in the school system, the more disengaged they become academically and intellectually. Social engagement is the only stable, high-engagement piece over the course of a student's school experience. Most students enjoy coming to school for much of their school career. When students enjoy the social aspects of school, it allows teachers to intervene in the academic and intellectual engagement pieces by paying attention to the elements of academic trust. Individual teachers can build on the social engagement most students feel about school by being the kind of teacher described above and applying some simple interventions that create an environment of academic trust.

Every teacher can get better at applying strategies that support even the most distrustful student so that they are more willing to become academically and intellectually engaged while in the classroom. Several strategies will be provided in Chapters 7 and 8. As teachers actualize the suggested attributes and implement the strategies, they will see the increased impact of academic trust in their students. Just how challenging is it to create this kind of learning environment?

Teaching Complexity and the Trust-Distrust Dilemma

Trust in our current educational systems is under attack on many fronts. Why is this so? Contemporary distrust of public education can be attributed, at least in part, to George Bernard Shaw. His well-known comment made in 1905, in his play, *Man and Superman*, epitomizes a popular belief about teaching that declares, "Those who can, do; those who can't, teach." implying that teaching is for those who are less able, less skilled, and less intelligent. Sadly, this disparaging comment continues to receive public support over 100 years later. Was Shaw right? The simple truth is no! It is virtually impossible to teach something you do not know. Just try it. Neither reading, mathematics, music, carpentry, medicine, law, engineering, or any other learning discipline can be taught by those who do not know and understand these disciplines. But just because someone knows and understands a discipline doesn't mean that they can teach it. Knowing something and being able to teach it are two very different things. Becoming an expert teacher requires a set of complex interactive skills, all of which are established upon the foundations of interpersonal and academic trust within a context of institutional trust, and all of which are learned over time. In addition, expert teaching requires an understanding of a specific discipline at all levels of Bloom's Revised Taxonomy (see Chapter 7), and an understanding of how to organize and scaffold the learning process for all levels of learners.

Classrooms are complex learning environments. Let's illustrate this complexity with the simple salesman problem as described by math professor Tyler Jarvis (2013). He explains that if the travelling salesman has three destinations to go to, there are six possible routes to be considered. Increase the number of destinations to four and the number of possible routes jumps to 24. Increase the number of destinations to ten and the possible routes to consider increases to 3,628,800. Finally, increase the number of destinations to 20—incidentally the number of students in a relatively small classroom—and the possible routes to consider completing the route grows to 2,432,902,008,176,640,000. This number reads 2 quintillion, 432 quadrillion, 902 trillion, 8 billion, 176 million, 640 thousand. This is the number of possible routes; the quickest is yet to be determined. This mathematical function is referred to as combinatorial explosion. Using the best 2013 computer to check just one billion routes to determine the fastest possible route would take the computer 77 years.

The Clay Mathematics Institute in Cambridge has offered a $1,000,000.00 prize to the first person who can offer an algorithm that would solve this travelling salesman problem within a reasonable amount of time. As of the writing of this book, it remains unclaimed. These huge numbers represent a simple math problem—what is the quickest route to take? However, the answer is a staggering size. The context of the travelling salesman problem would become infinitely more complicated if we threw in road construction, traffic congestion, mechanical breakdowns, wrong address deliveries, sick workers, accidents, upset clients and so forth. So, how does this apply to educational practice and its complexity?

For starters, many classrooms have upward of 30 or more students. Do the math for this number. What is the quickest route to get to every student who requires a different set of processes to help them learn the new materials, considering that real learning is difficult work? Navigating a multitude of interpersonal relationships laden with trust-distrust issues, while attempting to reach every single student academically and intellectually in the most efficient, effective manner is an activity that deserves to be acknowledged as extremely complex. More complicated than delivering packages and even more complicated than rocket science. Student self-confidence is fragile to say the least. Adult self-confidence is as fragile. Navigating the trust relationship dynamic of 30 teenagers in a small, closed space, each with varying degrees of social skill awareness and sensitivity, and the many difficult interrelationship connections between each of these 30 students, many of which can change from day-to-day, all while attempting to teach all of them new and difficult concepts simultaneously, is intricately sophisticated work. Now throw in the fact that it is 15 mins to lunch and many of these students didn't eat breakfast. Anyone who thinks teaching is easy and only for those who "can't do" have literally reduced the teaching learning process to a simple caricature.

The layers of professional challenge to create an entire school community of teaching expertise are more abstruse and sophisticated than is realized and understood by those who attempt to do so. This, in part, explains the amount of system failure to scale up and improve. As schools strive to scale up to move mediocre teachers to become good teachers and good teachers to become expert teachers, they become involved in an infinitely perplexing process. Truly coming to understand the complicated interrelated roles of interpersonal, institutional, and academic trust is key to this goal. The dynamic of trust and distrust inherent in any school system is often not clearly understood by those tasked with moving improvement forward. And as such, movement forward is too often stalled.

Trust and distrust issues continuously weave their way through contemporary public education discourse. The distrust phenomena are aptly illustrated by the following book review. In *Distrust and Educational Change*, Katherine Schultz argues that distrust—and the failure to recognize and address it—significantly contributes to the failure of policies meant to improve educational systems. In her work, Schultz identifies two detrimental forces, the first, top-down decision making and, the second, high-stakes external testing where she explains these tests are, "based on a premise of distrust by outsiders of local—or teachers'—knowledge of student progress, as well as a distrust of teachers' ability to accurately assess students' understandings. High-stakes tests are used not only to assess students in a manner that may not be connected to classroom instruction but can also be used to evaluate teachers." (https://www.edweek.org/leadership/opinion-there-is-rampant-distrust-in-education-heres-how-to-fix-that/2019/06). In addition, Thomas Hoerr writes, "Virtually all the education leaders that I know are people of wisdom and integrity. But too often they're operating in a climate of cynicism and distrust. What can be done?" (Hoerr, 2014). The point is that there is ample evidence to support the belief that trust in public education is under fire and that there are concerns about its ability to do the job it was designed to do. But even with systemic distrust in place, every individual teacher can still move forward within the walls of their own classroom in their desire to reach each of their students as they focus on how to leverage academic trust.

A Summary of Trust Before We Proceed

Trust is visceral. We all think it and feel it, often strongly, about who and what we should or should not trust. We know when we have it and when we do not. A trusted teacher is perceived to be competent, benevolent, a person of integrity, and empathetic. If teachers struggle with any of these attributes, they will struggle with developing trusting relationships with their students, and they will certainly be challenged to create an environment of academic trust in their classrooms. Despite the complexity of trust, students size up new teachers in about ten seconds.

All of us, including our students, simplify complex social contexts using heuristics to navigate them. We frame these complex social circumstances and make comparisons based upon previous experience. We often get it right, and sometimes we don't. Confirmation bias plays a key role in determining not only how we see events, but what we see in those events. Fundamentally, we see what we expect to see. A distrust perception filter really impacts how anyone interacts with systems, individuals, and learning environments.

Trust decisions take place in the brain, and how the brain works can be observed. The brain has automatic and controlled information processing systems. The automatic system is driven by emotion and intuition, is slow, less affected by cognitive load, sensitive to subliminal influences, insensitive to nuances and exceptions to the rule, and is a slow learner. The controlled system is driven by logic and reason, is fast, more affected by cognitive load, less affected by subliminal influences, sensitive to nuances, and is a fast learner. This dual processor system works—using the strengths from each system simultaneously—to make sense out of our environment to determine the level of trust warranted.

Trust is impacted by a combination of neurochemicals and perceptual factors that work together. Within the brain, the polyvagal system manages the three chemicals—oxytocin, vasopressin, and dopamine—as we wrestle with and decide personal trust decisions as determined by social context. There is a small percentage of individuals who have difficulty interpreting social context or feeling empathetic, which is possibly related to brain malformation, genetics, or hormone activation interfering with their ability to create and appropriately manage trusting relationships. This small population's influence within social environments can generate significant negative consequences.

Institutional trust works differently than interpersonal trust. Structural assurance and situational normality determine the level of institutional trust that individuals feel. If things in our world unfold as we believe they should, and the institutions around us function as we predict that they should, we tend to have high confidence in them and will trust them. The current COVID-19 pandemic and the 2020 US election have brought institutional trust into question, demonstrating its fragility as situational normality has been significantly impacted.

An operational definition of academic trust, along with a model, and a conceptual framework was introduced. Academic trust is driven by the beliefs and behaviours of individual teachers. Students interpret the actions of the teacher and then determine how much academic trust will be given to the teacher. If an acceptable standard is met, students will feel confident enough to trust that their teacher will offer helpful support. It is well known that if a student likes their teacher, that teacher will get more from their student than if the student does not like their teacher. Likeable teachers get more effort, cooperation, support, enjoyment, and more learning from their students. Likewise, if a student does not like the teacher, the teacher will get less of these behaviours. Developing academic trust is key to enlarging the instructional impact of teachers in their classrooms.

4

Teacher Control, Influence, and Concern

At the end of the day, you can't control the results;
you can only control your effort level
and your focus.
Ben Zobrist

No OTHER GROUP HAS MORE IMPACT ON STUDENT LEARNING THAN THAT OF teachers. Surely this should be the case, considering the time, energy, effort, and skill used to support young people in the development of their dreams and goals for their future. Many teachers hang around long enough to see their students become trades persons, public service workers, professionals, and yes, even their newest students' parents and grandparents. Teachers can often clearly remember these young ones on their first days of school, as tiny little children, and imagining what might become of them and what they might do with their lives.

In terms of the big picture, there are not a whole lot of things that any teacher has absolute control over except their power to decide what they will do within the walls of their own classroom. It is in this space where the magic happens. Most teachers are good, caring people. They spend countless hours prepping, teaching, and assessing their students' work and providing opportunities for their students to participate in extracurricular endeavours. In a single year, one teacher can donate hundreds of volunteer hours. Many educators do all that they do simply because they love helping young people and that is their reward. Teachers make a world of difference.

In regard to their instructional practice, teachers are often in control of their instructional and assessment planning. What are some of the behind the scenes work teachers engage in prior to stepping into the classroom? Their planning includes curriculum selection processes, meaning how they synthesize the mandated curriculum and make decisions about the content and processes that students must know, the things that are good to know, and the remaining things that would be nice for students to know, related to that curriculum. Not every learning outcome is of equal importance in investment of time and energy, thus content and curriculum decisions are made. Yearly, weekly, daily, and unit lesson plans are all a part of the instructional process. Generally, teachers can choose the instructional strategies and approaches that will be implemented in their day-to-day practice, along with the resources that will support these instructional approaches. They also make choices between direct or indirect instruction; individual or group activities; listening or speaking; reading or writing; using a lot or a little time; presentation, paper or quiz assessments; and how each assessment will be designed, with some exceptions. How much this assignment will be weighted, how much formative versus summative assessment will be used, and where and when these will take place, are all often carefully determined. Considerations for differentiated instruction, Universal Design for Learning, backward planning, and student practice are all part of the instructional planning process, to name just a few. While all this teacher planning is essential to good instructional practice, it does not necessarily guarantee successful or exceptional instructional practice as identified by Shelley Harwayne in Chapter 3. Success in the instructional piece requires careful planning; however, careful planning does not guarantee instructional success. The fact is that instructional impact begins in the hallway. Teachers need to create a personal relationship with each and every student. They can do this by simply chatting with them in the hall as they welcome them into their classroom. What are the students interested in? Find out.

Circles of Control, Influence, and Concern

The following discussion focuses on placing the proper context on the things that teachers directly control that influence student learning and engagement, and where instructional expertise and capacity growth matter most. Figure 3 helps teachers see what they can control, what they have influence on, and to identify their concerns for which they can do little about.

All teachers have limits over what they can control and influence. However, the things that they do have control and influence over are typically connected to their ability to build their own capacity to impact student learning directly. Teachers typically have control over communicating and implementing the

Figure 3

Circles of Instructional Control, Influence, and Concern

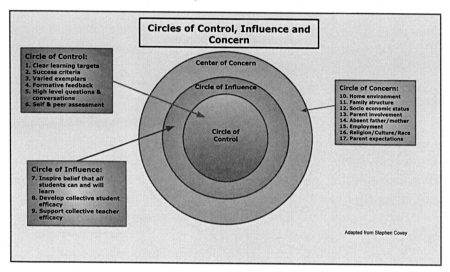

clear learning targets; establishing success criteria; providing clear exemplars, formative feedback, and high-level questions and conversations; and promoting self and peer assessment.

Every teacher can build their capacity with these teacher activities individually, or collectively with a cohort of other teachers; however, each teacher is responsible for the performance of these activities within the walls of their own classroom. A specific way to spread influence and build academic trust is to represent a personal belief that all students can and will learn. This can be practiced by modelling inclusive behaviour in classrooms and schools. Every teacher also has influence on developing collective student and teacher efficacy. Teachers influence—instead of control—these processes simply because each teacher must rely on the willingness of others to participate in the processes. As teachers build capacity in each area of practice, they will impact student learning and academic trust more robustly.

As compelling as these processes are, the teacher or other individuals can choose not to support the processes and indeed work against them. Teachers have no control over students assigned to their classes or the adults that they may work with. As such, teachers will have students that are so challenging to work with, for numerous reasons, that nurturing a relationship of academic trust may take more time, effort, or skill than anticipated. How willing and how skilled individual teachers are in creating interpersonal trust and motivating others to buy into collective efforts varies and can influence other participants to either accept or reject attempts to work collaboratively. Building the capacity to navigate complex relationships is something all teachers can learn to do. And in doing so, they can realize success with complex, challenging behaviours that come from their students and their colleagues.

As teachers build capacity within the areas over which they have control, they can exert more influence over the more collaborative influencer activities. Academic trust is built in the day-to-day interactions between the teacher and the student one interaction at a time. As teachers organize and lead what happens in the classroom, they can create an atmosphere of collective support amongst students as these students work together to master the learning goals. As teachers work with each other in determining and implementing the school's vision, mission, goals, and instructional alignment processes, they build collective teacher efficacy. Connecting time, effort, energy, and focus to those things that teachers have control over and have reasonable influence on allows the right things to be chosen, at the right time, for the right purposes. Those working in schools often find themselves having to choose between too many good things. Being focused on your purpose and your vision allows you to say no to those things that are good, but not necessarily better or best for your current time and place. Thus, focusing on those things that teachers have control over and building capacity in these areas will ensure a greater instructional impact.

5

Teacher Impact— Learning Targets, Criteria, and Exemplars

Make your intentions clear. The universe does not respond well to uncertainty.
Joe Duncan, Founder
of Before5am

HOW SUCCESSFUL IS MY TEACHING? THIS IS THE MOST IMPORTANT QUESTION that every teacher needs to ask themselves. If they want to become expert teachers, they need to continue with this line of questioning about their teaching practice. How do I measure success? Why do I teach the way that I do? Why do I prepare instruction the way that I do? Why do I instruct students the way that I do? Why do I assess students the way that I do? Am I improving as a teacher? How do I know? What is the personal lens used to determine the answers to these questions? These are not easy questions to answer. They require the asker to become aware of their implicit beliefs, biases, and motivations connected to why they do what they do as a teacher. These implicit beliefs, biases, and motivations drive behaviour, and behaviour is manifested in what we are willing, or not willing to do to become a better teacher. If you are a normal teacher, and most teachers are severely normal, there will be things in your behaviour that will get in the way of you becoming a more expert teacher, most of which functions at the subconscious level.

Research demonstrates that implicit biases, that are subconscious, will manifest themselves in behaviour despite stated beliefs in opposition to this behaviour. Notwithstanding best efforts, Bruce Lipton (2008) explains:

The subconscious mind, one of the most powerful information processes known, specifically observes both the surrounding world and the body's internal awareness, reads the cues, and immediately engages previously acquired (learned) behaviors—all without the help, supervision, or even awareness of the conscious mind.

The unconscious mind receives, stores, and sends information, akin to an automatic data manager for our life experiences. The unconscious—more than the conscious mind—controls our daily decisions and actions, including how we relate to other people. John Powell explains that only two percent of our emotional cognition is conscious; the remainder lives in our unconscious networks, where implicit biases reside (Safir, 2016). Unless teachers are willing to examine what they do, in terms of their behaviour, and enlist the support of outside observers to help uncover their implicit beliefs, biases, and motivations, their biases will be difficult, if not impossible to come to know, understand, evaluate, and act upon.

There are many examples of unconscious bias that occur in schools. Teachers will readily recognize the following examples: Boys are more out of control in classrooms than girls. The students that teachers like will get better grades. Boys are better at math than girls. Students who speak up more in classroom discussions are smarter than those who do not.

Every teacher has unconscious beliefs that drive their behaviours with regard to the different cliques found within most schools, such as the jocks, geeks, cheerleaders, gamers, hipsters, stoners, troublemakers, class clowns, gangsters, ghetto kids, racial groups, foreigners, and so forth. Each of these group stereotypes become embedded unconscious biases, whether for good or for bad.

On a larger scale, unconscious biases often manifest themselves in school systems where they drive discipline, inclusive education, and student tracking policy, all of which can be unconsciously influenced by factors such as race, gender, wealth inequality, family connections, and geographical location. Teacher mindsets and beliefs are unconsciously co-opted by the systems within which they serve, impacting how they see groups of students within the school. This unconscious set of beliefs manifests itself in the dominant discourse adopted by teachers that may "diminish, underestimate, or even pathologize" (Safir, 2016) the students.

It is hoped that teachers will be able to recognize some of their biases and ask themselves how their biases may be affecting their goal of becoming an expert teacher. Expert teachers are open to self and peer examination of their practice to get better. To become better, evidence of teacher underperformance must be clearly visible to the teacher. A certain amount of vulnerability is required for teacher improvement to take place. At the end of the day, the teacher and the student must be on the same page with regard to task clarity and task processes. It does not matter how well a teacher understands their discipline if their students don't get what it is they are trying to teach. What matters is how clearly a teacher can communicate their understanding of the subject to their students. It is at this intersection that teacher expertise matters most, and where academic trust is established.

So how does a teacher measure their success? Teacher success can be measured by how many of their students are able to clearly understand the tasks assigned to them, and how well they are able to perform the task processes required to be successful. They measure their success by how successful their students are. Becoming crystal clear on communicating to their students the learning targets, criteria, and exemplars—so that task clarity is optimized—is paramount to becoming an expert teacher. Teachers need to ask their students—in straightforward ways—what it is they understand and don't understand about the learning targets and then help fill in the gaps. If a high level of academic trust is present, their students will tell them. Let's be clear that although these described teacher activities are often seen as basic, they are also foundational to student understanding and learning and are not in anyway simple or trivial. They cannot be passed over as optional because it is impossible to have good instructional practice without these practices. To become an expert teacher, a person could spend a lifetime striving to perfect them. This is, in fact, where within-school variability resides. Closing the achievement gap can only happen in classrooms where teachers reach and teach every student. The remainder of this book provides support in how to effectively do this.

Figure 4 provides a model that empowers teachers to critique their capacity in six practices that impact student engagement and learning. It requires teachers to examine their beliefs about student learning capacity, and it points teachers in the direction of expanding their capacity to influence their students and colleagues more powerfully. Figure 4 conceptualizes the work of the teacher in the classroom and the practices they can focus on to increase their impact on student learning and academic trust.

Figure 4
Teacher! What is Your Instructional Impact?

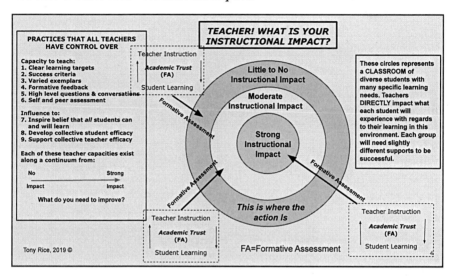

The three circles represent the diverse classroom and the levels of impact that typical classroom teaching has on students. Some students are impacted strongly, others moderately, while some very little or not at all. Every teacher has many strengths and some areas that require capacity building.

The first six practices that all teachers have control over come from a study that examined the ability of school principals and teachers to work together to build their professional capacity (Rice, 2016). The chart that was used to track these first six teacher practices was referred to as *The Assessment of Learning Journey,* and the data collected from the study clearly supported the finding that when principals and teachers collaborated to build their capacity, they were more successful. The study, and a portion of its data, will be shared in Appendix B.

When reviewing the practices identified in the box on the left, teachers can rate themselves on a scale from unconvincing evidence to compelling evidence. As part of the self-assessment process, teachers must be able to identify the evidence that supports their claim. If they have compelling evidence, can it be produced or demonstrated? If the evidence is unconvincing, can they identify how they plan to move to the next level?

Finally, as teachers interact with their students, providing differentiated formative assessment experiences for them, are they also developing an academic trust relationship with each student and monitoring this impact? As teachers develop their capacity, they expand their impact and control of the learning environment.

This book provides several charts that support teachers in identifying and tracking areas of growth within the teaching practices that they have control or influence over. After identifying an area that a teacher chooses to build capacity in, they can focus their attention on this teacher practice and track their growth. Six of these charts are improved upon from *The Assessment for Learning Journey* original chart. There are additional resources that expand on feedback and metacognition in support of teacher practice. Each of the teacher practices are grade and subject independent. In this chapter, we will discuss the first three practices.

Practice 1: Building Capacity with Learning Targets

Practice Chart 1 allows teachers to analyse the clarity that they bring to the intended learning goals for their students so that these goals are clearly communicated to their students. Rick Stiggins shares a teaching reality. He declares, "The single most common barrier to sound classroom assessment is the teacher's lack of vision of appropriate achievement targets within the subjects they are supposed to teach." The clearer the teacher is, the clearer the students can be in grappling with new learning content. If neither the teacher nor students are clear about what the learning target is, how will either know if they are close to hitting the target? Robert Marzano has stated, "Students who can identify what they are learning significantly outscore those who cannot." Students are clear because the teacher is clear. It is that simple.

Learning goals should identify what is to be learned, be linked to the overall and specific expectations to be addressed, be connected to a big idea, and identify incremental steps to build student knowledge and skills. Learning goals also need to use clear, concise language, be student-friendly and grade-appropriate, use verbs that describe specific and observable actions and are stated from a student's perspective, such as, "We are learning to …" James Popham (2003) has concluded, "Teachers who truly understand what they want their students to accomplish will almost surely be more instructionally successful than teachers whose understanding of hoped-for student accomplishments are murky."

Practice Chart 1
Learning Targets

1. LEARNING TARGETS

Step 1: Rate your current level of learning target competence.
Step 2: What evidence supports your claim?
Step 3: What evidence will take you to the next level?

Clear LEARNING TARGETS (outcomes/competencies)	Unconvincing	Simplistic	Convincing	Compelling
Teachers can confidently interpret and prioritize learner outcomes from the program of studies (i.e., can identify enduring understandings, important to know and do, worth being familiar with)				
Students are informed of the learner outcomes				
Students can explain what they are there to learn (i.e., can articulate the learning target)				
Learner targets/outcomes are visible (i.e., stated, shared, shown) throughout the learning process (e.g., plans, assignments, assessment/ evaluation tools, gradebooks, etc.)				
Teachers gather a variety of assessment evidence to measure achievement in relation to the outcomes (i.e., triangulates written, oral, and presentation evidence)				

Due to time constraints, every learning goal in many curricula cannot be specifically taught, so teachers need to be able to distinguish between those that are essential, those that are important, and those that are worth being familiar with. This seems simple enough to do; however, experience demonstrates that when you have a group of teachers working together to decide this scope, every learning outcome becomes essential. Being clear on what is being taught and why, and how it fits into the bigger picture supports students as they seek to clear up the cognitive dissonance created by all new learning experiences.

Practice 2: Building Capacity with Criteria

Practice Chart 2 allows teachers to see how well they communicate with their students about the quality of the students' work. "In assessing the quality of a student's work or performance, the teacher must possess a concept of quality appropriate to the task and be able to judge the student's work in relation to that concept" (Sadler, 1989). Success criteria identify what it is that students need to know, understand, and do related to the learning target and how close they are to the target. The criteria act as a guide for student learning and support the student in completing the assignment by helping the student to know what to look for. The parts of the criteria checklist identify the next steps toward completion of the assignment. If the student is missing something, that becomes the next step.

A simple example to illustrate success criteria would be grade six students assigned to develop their paragraph writing skills. The learning target would be: students will write a paragraph paying attention to external and internal paragraph structures. The success criteria would be an identification of those external and internal paragraph structures.

External structure criteria:
- Is there a clear topic sentence outlining your writing purpose?
- Are there several supporting ideas clearly connected to your topic sentence?
- Are these supporting ideas written in their proper order? (chronological, order of importance, sequence, etc.)
- Is there a concluding sentence that connects the supporting details to the topic sentence? And/or does the concluding sentence transition to a next topic or make a point connected to the topic sentence?

Internal structure criteria:
- Is each sentence complete with capitalization and punctuation?
- Are the appropriate transition and sequencing words used for the type of paragraph? (compare and contrast, sequence, list, chronology, etc.)
- Are interesting word choices and literary devices used to create a clear picture of your ideas? (similes, metaphors, hyperbole, repetition, etc.)

If the student writer can show evidence and check all these questions off, they know that they have met the success criteria for the learning target.

Practice Chart 2
Criteria

2. CRITERIA

Step 1: Rate your current level of criteria competence.
Step 2: What evidence supports your claim?
Step 3: What evidence will take you to the next level?

Development of CRITERIA (i.e., what a student has to know and be able to do in order to achieve the outcome)	Unconvincing	Simplistic	Convincing	Compelling
Teachers confidently turn learner outcomes into success criteria				
Students understand the criteria required to meet an outcome				
Criteria is (to some degree) co-developed with students to support the development of their understanding of it				
Criteria for summative assessment is transparent to students (i.e., assessment tool is available from the outset)				

Practice 3: Building Capacity with Exemplars

Practice Chart 3 allows teachers to see if they provide students with examples of the learning goals' intended product (exemplars), illustrating the range of student work from what is considered acceptable to what is considered exemplary. Exemplars are aligned to the learning goal and the success criteria, and they provide a model for students to work from in developing their own work on a similar task. Exemplars begin with the end in mind. Exemplars can be a demonstration, conversation, sample, product, or other model.

Exemplars help to make complex success criteria more comprehensible to students and ensure standards across time and cohorts of students, contributing toward equity and fairness. Providing opportunity for student-to-student conversations about the quality of exemplars can increase student

Practice Chart 3
Exemplars

3. EXEMPLARS

Step 1: Rate your current level of exemplar competence.
Step 2: What evidence supports your claim?
Step 3: What evidence will take you to the next level?

Use of EXEMPLARS (i.e., can be a demonstration, conversation, sample product, etc.)	Unconvincing	Simplistic	Convincing	Compelling
Students have access to examples of varied levels of performance in order to compare their own work				
Teachers are confident about when and how in the learning process to scaffold learning with exemplars				
Student-to-student conversations about quality support their learning about high-quality responses				

awareness of the cognitive skills required to construct high-quality responses (Rashid-Doubell et al., 2018). Examples of exemplars abound with a quick internet search. For instance, here is a URL from Alberta Education providing a sample from a grade three learning assessment in literacy:

https://education.alberta.ca/media/3386094/19-gr3lit-exemplars-2016_redfox.pdf

In addition, LearnAlberta.ca, a government of Alberta website resource, has a great dropdown menu that provides writing exemplars from grades 1-12 that are benchmarked from level one to level five. The exemplars are provided for teacher use but can also be used for student exemplars.

Creating Impact with Appropriate Feedback

An inability to tolerate feedback is an inability
to allow yourself personal growth.
Columbus State University
Leadership Institute

CHAPTER 6 FOCUSES SPECIFICALLY ON THE TOPIC OF PROVIDING EFFECTIVE formative feedback to students. It begins with the teacher self-assessment chart and leads to a discussion about *The Power of Feedback* from Hattie and Timperley (2007). This discussion is included so that each teacher is clear about what effective formative assessment looks like and does not look like. This understanding is imperative so that next steps include clarity about the task, clarity about the processes, and clarity about self-regulation strategies, and is clearly understood and applied uniformly by all teachers. Hattie and Timperley's paper is foundational to any discussion about providing effective feedback to students so that they can close the gap between their current work and clearly hitting the learning target.

Practice 4: Building Capacity with Feedback

Practice Chart 4 is about teachers checking in to see how clear their instructions are about the task, and the task processes, and to see how well students are self-regulating as they address new challenging learning. Are teachers providing useful information about performance?

Formative feedback is timely. It is applied when students need support, and it supports students moving to what comes next, as a matter of course. Providing appropriate task, process, and self-regulation feedback and clarity to students is one of the most powerful practices teachers can apply.

Practice Chart 4
Feedback

4. FEEDBACK				
Step 1: Rate your current level of feedback competence. Step 2: What evidence supports your claim? Step 3: What evidence will take you to the next level?				
Provides useful information about performance FEEDBACK in relation to the learner outcomes and criteria (clarity about the task, task processes, and self-regulation)	Unconvincing	Simplistic	Convincing	Compelling
Is descriptive (articulates what is on track and what needs attention)				
Helps guide the next step in learning (i.e., closes the gap)				
Next steps include clarity about the task, clarity about the processes, and clarity about self-regulation strategies				
Is frequent, timely and varied (i.e., both oral and written)				
Comes from peers, teachers, and self				

Figure 5 is a model created by Hattie and Timperley (2007). Their model provides the clearest, most specific, and effective feedback language that can be used by all teachers and students so that they can efficiently communicate about what it is that the learner needs to do next to move closer to the learning target. The model aligns the learning target (where the learner is going), with how the learner gets there (the strategies and processes), and where to go next (the success criteria). It concludes with four levels of feedback, the first three of which are very useful. The last one—which happens to be the one most often used by teachers—has little to no or negative value because it provides no direction for next steps.

Figure 6 identifies the three feedback questions: Where am I going? How am I going? Where to next? Each of these questions includes a set of guiding statements that provide clear, specific direction for teachers to apply. Following the three questions are the four feedback levels: task; process; self-regulation; and self, and a similar set of statements for teacher use and clarity.

Figure 5

A Model of Feedback to Enhance Learning

Purpose:
To reduce discrepancies between current understandings/
performance and a desired goal (the learning outcome)

↓

The discrepancy can be reduced by:
Students:
Increased effort and employment of more effective strategies
OR
Abandoning, blurring, or lowering the goals (student
anticipates no success, undesirable state) *

Teachers:
Providing appropriate challenging and specific goals
Assisting students to reach them through effective learning strategies and feedback

↓

Effective feedback answers three questions:
1. Where am I going? (the goals)   Feed Up
2. How am I going? (strategies/processes)   Feed Back
3. Where to next? (hint: check criteria)   Feed Forward

↓

Each feedback question works at four levels:

↓   ↓   ↓   ↓

Task level	**Process level**	**Self-regulation level**	**Self level**
How well task levels are understood/ performed	The main processes needed to understand/ perform tasks	Self-monitoring, directing, and regulating of actions	Personal evaluations and affect (usually positive) about the learner

*Note: *Some strategies to reduce the gap are less productive. Students may abandon goals and thus eliminate any gap, and this often leads to non-engagement in the pursuit of further goals (Bandura, 1982; Mikulincer, 1988; Steinberg, 1996). They may choose to blur the goals, combining them with so many others that after performing, they can pick and choose those goals they attained and ignore the others. Alternatively, students can change the standard by setting less-challenging goals, accepting performance far below their capabilities as satisfactory. (p. 87) From The Power of Feedback Model (Hattie & Timperley, 2007)*

Figure 6

Feedback Chart: Addressing & Implementing the Three Feedback Questions &
the Four Levels in Classroom Assessment Practice

Feedback Chart: Addressing & Implementing the Three Feedback Questions & the Four Levels in Classroom Assessment Practice	
Where am I going?	• The learning goal is clear to the teacher and the students • The students are committed to the learning goal • The students understand the success criteria (a model of success) • The student has the necessary instruction
How Am I Going?	• The students have the appropriate skills and strategies to meet the goal (capacity) • The appropriate scaffolding is in place for students to be guided
Where to Next?	• The student uses success criteria to determine next steps • The student is aware that the topic goes deeper and broader • The student is aware of the next connected challenges • The student is aware of the next strategies & processes • The student is aware of the next level of self-regulation
Task level How well task levels are understood/ performed	• Feedback addresses faulty interpretations • Feedback is task related and not self-level related • Feedback is directed toward the appropriate level of performance • Feedback is not confused with marks or grades • Feedback is focused on the correct information • Feedback is connected to the processes underlying the task and how to extend the task • Feedback supports student error detection strategies leading to self-feedback

To emphasize the importance of students engaging in the work of building their capacity for employing metacognitive strategies, a sample chart is included with the purpose of providing clarity about this work. Just as feedback has a high effect size of 0.7 with regard to impacting student achievement, metacognition strategies have an equally strong impact. To be clear, effect size is a measure of how powerful a specific teaching strategy is in impacting student learning. Hattie (2009) has defined an effect size of 0.4 as one that guarantees one year's student growth in one year's time. While almost everything teachers do in their classrooms to teach has a positive impact on student learning, the important question is: how much impact? Teachers are

Process level The main processes needed to understand/perform tasks	• Feedback is specific to the task processes or to relating and extending the task • Feedback supports students in their own error detection and how to correct them • Feedback acts as a cueing mechanism (using a graphic organizer) that leads to more effective information search and strategy application • Feedback enhances deeper learning
Self-regulation level Self-monitoring, directing, and regulating of actions	• Feedback provides opportunities for students to review and evaluate their abilities, knowledge states, and cognitive strategies through a variety of self-monitoring processes. (metacognitive strategies) • Feedback provides opportunities for students to monitor their ongoing learning through planning, correcting mistakes, and using fix-up strategies, evaluating their level of understanding, their effort and strategies used on tasks, their attributions, and opinions of others about their performance, and their improvement in relation to their goals and expectations • Feedback allows students to assess their performance relative to others' goals and the global aspects of their performance • Students know how and when to seek and receive feedback from others and feel positive about this process • Feedback is clearly connected to student performance and students can see how to improve their performance
Self level Personal evaluations and affect (usually positive) about the learner	• Teachers avoid this type of feedback • Teachers are aware of the "reputational lens"* students function from and plan accordingly • Teachers reinforce the beliefs that time on task, effort, and student skill sets determine success

*Note: *Reputational lens refers to how a student sees themselves in relation to their peers. "I want to be seen as a good student" or "I want to be seen as a bad student."*

encouraged to select the more powerful strategies to support student learning and to remove less impactful strategies. As teachers improve at providing specific and more supportive feedback at the task, process, and self-regulation levels, and include student instruction and practice with metacognition strategies, these combined practices will have an even greater impact on student achievement and engagement.

Figure 7 provides a framework for teacher and student use. The more clearly students can answer these questions, the more success they will have mastering the learning targets.

Figure 7

Sample Self-Questions to Promote Student Metacognition About Learning

Sample self-questions to promote student metacognition about learning			
Activity	Planning	Monitoring	Evaluating
Class session	• What are the goals of the class session going to be? • What do I already know about this topic? • How should I best prepare for the class session? • Where should I sit and what could I be doing (or not doing) to best support my learning during class? • What questions do I already have about this topic that I want to find out more about?	• What insights am I having as I experience this class session? What is confusing to me? • What questions are arising for me during the class session? Am I writing them down somewhere? • Do I find this interesting? Why or why not? How could I make this material personally relevant? • Can I distinguish important information from details? If not, how will I figure this out?	• What was today's class session about? • What did I hear today that is in conflict with my prior understanding? • How did the ideas of today's class session relate to previous class sessions? • What do I need to actively go and do now to get my questions answered and my confusions clarified? • What did I find most interesting about class today?
Active-learning task and/or homework assignment	• What is the instructor's goal in having me do this task? • What are all the things I need to do to successfully accomplish this task? • What resources do I need to complete the task? How will I make sure I have them? • How much time do I need to complete the task? • If I have done something like this before, how could I do a better job this time?	• What strategies am I using that are working well or not working well to help me learn? • What other resources could I be using to complete this task? What action can I take to get these? • What is most challenging for me about this task? What is most confusing? • What could I do differently mid-assignment to address these challenges and confusions?	• To what extent did I successfully accomplish the goals of the task? • To what extent did I use resources available to me? • If I were the instructor, what would I identify as strengths of my work and flaws in my work? • When I do an assignment or task like this again, what do I want to remember to do differently? What worked well for me that I could use next time?

Quiz or exam	• What strategies will I use to study (e.g., study groups, problem sets, evaluating text figures, challenging myself with practice quizzes, and/or going to office hours and review sessions)? • How much time do I plan on studying? Over what period of time and for how long each time I sit down do I need to study? • Which aspects of the course material would be best to spend more or less time on, based on my current understanding?	• To what extent am I being systematic in my studying of all the material for the exam? • To what extent am I taking advantage of all the learning supports available to me? • Am I struggling with my motivation to study? If so, do I remember why I am taking this course? • Which of my confusions have I clarified? How was I able to get them clarified? • Which confusions remain and how am I going to get them clarified?	• What about my exam preparation worked well that I would like to remember to do next time? • What did not work so well that I would rather not do next time or that I could change? • What questions did I answer correctly? Why? How did my answer compare with the suggested correct answer? • What questions did I not answer correctly? Why? What confusions do I have that I still need to clarify?
Overall course	• Why is it important to learn the material in this course? • How does success in this course relate to my career or life goals? • How am I going to actively monitor my learning in this course? • What do I most want to learn from this course? • What do I want to be able to do by the end of this course?	• In what ways is the teaching in this course supportive of my learning? How could I maximize this? • In what ways is the teaching in this course not supportive of my learning? How could I compensate for or change this? How interested am I in this course? How confident am I in my learning? What could I do to increase my interest and confidence?	• What will I still remember five years from now that I learned in this course? • What advice would I give a friend about how to learn the most in this course? • If I were to teach this course, how would I change it? • What have I learned about how I learn during this course that I could use in my future courses, my career, or other applications?

Inspired by Ertmer and Newby (1996), Schraw (1998), and Coutinho (2007).

Used with permission from https://www.lifescied.org/doi/full/10.1187/cbe.12-03-0033#T1

Chapter 6 has scrutinized the topic of formative feedback. This type of feedback is about supporting students in improving the quality of their work by helping them to be clear about the task they are undertaking, and the processes required to complete the task. In practical terms, feedback has come to mean different things to different teachers. Hattie and Timperely provide a useful model for creating a uniform understanding about the kind of ideas that provide clarity around the topic. Their model delivers what teachers need to understand so that they can more effectively support student learning. Just as learning targets need to be clear, providing feedback about how to hit those targets needs to be just as clear. Appropriate feedback requires students to be thinking about their thinking. Student self-examination is an excellent example of the highest order of thinking they can do—therefore, it needs to be modelled and supported as a learning outcome. Providing students with a tool, such as the chart of sample self-questions to promote student metacognition about learning, is an excellent support for them and teachers as well.

7

The Impact of Questioning and Conversations

Knowledge is having the right answer. Intelligence is asking the right questions.
Unknown

QUESTIONING IS THE SECOND MOST DOMINANT TEACHING ACTIVITY AFTER teacher talk, and teachers can ask students up to 100 questions per hour (Cotton, 1989; Mohr, 1998). That said, up to 80% of those questions will be lower-level recall and procedural questions rather than higher-level analysis, evaluation, and creative questions (Brualdi, 1998; Wilen, 1991). Furthermore, as teachers get better at questioning students, they in turn can benefit greatly from examining the questions that students ask each other (Hattie et al., 1998). Student questions reveal what they are thinking about and not thinking about, and what they think about is what they will learn. Training in questioning matters, and teachers are open to getting better at questioning when given an opportunity (Hattie, 2009).

This section will offer a holistic approach to building teacher capacity to mobilize the Q&A strategy more productively. First, three Q&A entanglements that undermine student engagement and the development of academic trust will be considered. By making minor tactical adjustments, teachers will quickly experience how much more impact they can have on student engagement and academic trust. Secondly, a look at just who is in the classroom and how to address this student diversity more effectively regarding the Q&A will be explored. Finally, a systematic approach to the Q&A will be provided that will support new and experienced teachers in enhancing their Q&A instructional impact across all grades and subjects. Bolstering Q&A instructional impact is a teacher capacity priority that can be quickly accomplished.

9

Practice 5: Building Capacity with Questioning and Conversations

Practice Chart 5 encourages teachers to go beyond the typical Q&A that gets the ball rolling in terms of classroom interactions among students and between teacher and students.

Practice Chart 5
Questioning and Conversations

5. QUESTIONING AND CONVERSATIONS				
Step 1: Rate your current level of questioning/conversation competence. Step 2: What evidence supports your claim? Step 3: What evidence will take you to the next level?				
QUESTIONING and CONVERSATIONS	Unconvincing	Simplistic	Convincing	Compelling
Teachers confidently lead discussions that promote high levels of cognition (critical thinking, problem solving, analysis, evaluation, creation)				
Questioning techniques are used to engage all students—not just a few—in thinking and discussion related to the outcomes				
Summative assessment questions match the level of cognition of the learner outcome they are attempting to measure				
In a typical school day, students are actively and frequently involved in outcome-aligned collaborative work with peers, including providing constructive peer feedback				
Teachers purposefully apply Q&A strategies that are supportive of the disengaged student to build confidence				

First, to get the most from the practice chart assessment, there are three pitfalls that need to be understood. Very young students figure out the winners and losers in their own classrooms as they casually observe the student/teacher interactions that they are exposed to. It is at the intersection of the Q&A that academic trust most often breaks down for too many students. How does this happen?

Pitfall 1: The Low-Hanging Fruit

Typically, a teacher may begin today's lesson by reviewing yesterday's topic because there is often a connection. They begin, "Who knows such and such about yesterday's topic?" Generally, the younger the group of students, the more hands that will go up. Younger students are excited to participate, seek teacher and peer attention, and getting the correct answer to the question is a secondary motivation for many younger students. Thus, the typical strategy of throwing a question out to the entire class is not as effective as it could be. For these students, being first and being recognized are powerful motivators beyond getting the question correct.

The older the group of students, the fewer hands that will go up. Why is that? In the older grades, the hands that go up are from those who are confident that they know the answer. Seeking teacher attention and not knowing the answer is a minefield few experienced students venture into. In older grades, attention seekers get their attention in other ways—not by looking stupid trying to answer questions they do not know the answer to. Those who do know the answers are the ones in the centre circle (strong instructional impact) of Figure 4 in Chapter 5. These students exude social, academic, and intellectual confidence because they have figured out the teacher and their instructional approach, their schooling purpose, and how they learn. The moderately impacted students do well enough, but they do not always know why, and they are less willing to take the chance of putting their hand up. Their moderate success is still a mystery to them. They haven't made the solid connection between effort, consistency, and coming to know. There is still a bit of luck that they have enjoyed that helps explain their success. Those in the outer margins—the little to no impact students—are just lost and hope to get through the day without being called upon and embarrassed. They feel school is not for them, they do not trust teachers, they often do not relate to them, and they feel deep down that they are not very smart. Their past school experience has proven that to them. Academic trust is completely missing from their educational experience. Thus, those who put their hands up in the older grades are those of the low-hanging fruit variety. There will be few surprises for teachers working in this orchard.

Pitfall 2: Fight, Flight, or Freeze

Another typical Q&A scenario is the teacher checking in to see if students are understanding what it is that is being taught. A question goes out to the entire class, the confident learner puts their hand up, and they may or may not be called upon. Often, they are, and they typically get the answer correct and their belief about themselves continues to be confirmed that they are a good student, and this is likewise confirmed for the teacher. However, it can be the case that the teacher will ask a student that they know was not paying attention, or one they know struggles a little bit. The results are predictable. Those not paying attention don't know the answer; therefore, what they believe about themselves—that they are not a good student—is confirmed, thus reinforcing their earlier behaviour of not paying attention. Those who struggle don't put up their hand because they are not confident, so when called upon, they immediately go into the fight, flight, or freeze part of their brain and cannot share the answer even if they know it. What they feel about themselves as a learner is confirmed—they are a poor student—and everyone knows it, including the teacher. This group of students does not know the answer and does not want to look ignorant in front of their peers, and they often resort to off-handed humour to entertain their peers and distract from their ignorance. They end up either censured, ignored and passed over, removed from class, or a classmate is solicited to help them, thus confirming their choice of strategy.

Pitfall 3: The Bermuda Triangle

The final Q&A situation is referred to by Hattie as the Bermuda Triangle of teacher-student interactions. It is called this because everyone involved in the Q&A interaction gets lost. As described, the teacher calls upon a student to answer a question and the student does not know the answer. The teacher then calls on another student to please help the one who doesn't know the answer. In doing so, the teacher has just confirmed to the first student that they are not a good student, that they need help, and now everyone in the class knows this. The second student, by being asked to help out the first student, can either demonstrate their own superiority by answering correctly and be seen by their peers as a know-it-all or they can empathise with their fellow student and wish they were not involved in this embarrassing scenario. In addition, the teacher has just served notice to everyone in class that doesn't have a perfect understanding of the topic that they could be next to experience this same scenario, so watch out. One third of the students' brains in the class have just shut down and they want to ... you guessed it, run! Too often, the reluctant students, instead of thinking about the question under discussion, are thinking, "Please don't call on me. Please NO!" They would rather be hit by a bus than look ignorant in front of their peers or look like they care about real learning. The older the student, the more developed the façade of the disconnected student who resides in the margins of the classroom.

The three scenarios described above can purposely be reworked to avoid student disengagement. Too often, the low-hanging fruit is easily and quickly picked, and the real power of Q&A is abandoned for the perceived real work of learning. Deliberately targeting the higher-hanging fruit, the reluctant, disengaged participants, and engaging them safely in conversation about what they are learning, or what they are not learning, is the only way to develop, deepen, and expand the classroom culture of true academic trust. Students need to feel confident as learners and they need to trust that the teacher will never deliberately or unintentionally set them up for failure in front of their peers. Only confident capable students can handle this type of intellectual peer pressure without the fear factor taking over.

Extroverts and Introverts

There is a diversity found in every classroom that is seldom considered in terms of Q&A impact. As stated earlier, the ranking of winners and losers in the classroom—by the students themselves—begins at a very early age, almost entirely in the students' first year of formal schooling. Some of these young children purposefully jostle for position for teacher favour, and favour within and between their peers. However, significant numbers of students do not. A lot of jostling takes place during the teacher and student Q&A times. Teachers purposefully watch to see who is willing and who is unwilling to answer their questions, and they strive to expand this pool of willing participants. This is not a bad thing. Evidence of this desired teacher outcome is provided by many teachers in report card comments like the following:

"Should participate more in class discussions."

"Would do better if they participated in class discussions more often."

"Their reluctance to participate in class discussions tends to hold them back."

Student willingness to purposefully refrain from class discussion is seen by many educators as an academic weakness that needs to be repaired. There is a basic assumption that all children should want to participate in class discussions.

When teachers become more aware of the individual personality differences in their students as introverts and extroverts, they will be able to support them more appropriately in how to become engaged in Q&A. The extrovert has a huge advantage in the struggle to gain favour in the classroom. Extroverts are generally energized by social situations, while introverts are exhausted by them. Extroverts love to talk in front of an audience, the bigger the better, while introverts do not enjoy talking in front of crowds because they do not desire nor want the attention. Extroverts are very open and willing to share with everyone, while introverts do not like to be open and share, particularly in front of larger groups. Introverts are very selective and often are willing to share their best ideas only in small groups where they are less uncomfortable. Extroverts enjoy solving problems through group discussion and collaboration, while introverts prefer problem solving in very small groups and only when they are comfortable with the group members. Extroverts tend to be more confident in front of a crowd, while introverts are not confident in front of a crowd. Finally, extroverts are seen as friendly and very approachable, while introverts are not necessarily seen as friendly or approachable because they prefer to stay under the radar. Clearly, the extrovert draws the teacher's attention more quickly and easily and more often, likely impacting relationship building in a positive manner, while the introvert who does not do these things impacts relationship building with a different result. How different are these two types of personalities and what are the very real outcomes in the dynamic classroom?

Most students are neither entirely extroverted nor wholly introverted. While there are extremes, these would be rare; however, all students have a proclivity toward one or the other. Being aware of these very real personality predispositions is an important teacher tool, particularly when it comes to classroom Q&A and making decisions about academic ability.   Many children are naturally introverted, and this natural personality trait is largely ignored. In his work, psychologist Jonathan Cheek describes four types of introversion and alludes to more. Not all children care to gain favour with their teacher or their peers if it requires them to act in a manner described as being extroverted, simply because they are not. Cheek describes four kinds of introversion: social, thinking, anxious and restrained (or reserved).

The *social introvert* is often identified as the 'shy' student. In reality, this student prefers solitude and if they do not experience solitude there is a price they pay in terms of actual physical, mental, and emotional exhaustion. Preferring solitude appears to be a required survival mechanism linked to a personality characteristic that they did not choose. Teachers can work with these students one-on-one or in small groups and they can design opportunities for questioning experiences that help determine what they think about and what they are learning.

The *thinking introvert* is often seen as the daydreamer—the student who doesn't always pay attention. In fact, they were paying attention when something came up in the classroom Q&A discussion that sent them down a segued path of personal interest, creativity, and imagination. Instead of reprimanding them for not paying attention, it would be more profitable to ask these students what they were thinking about and what prompted them to go in that direction. Imagination and creativity are highly sought after 21st-century skills and when engaged in, these students should be gently prompted to share how the current discussion helped them to make connections in a different line of reasoning and then gently redirected back to the topic under discussion, all without judgement.

The *anxious introvert* is mistakenly viewed as the student that lacks confidence. However, they can do very well when it comes to performance on tests and individual assignments and when working alone. Their anxiety has little to do with intelligence or potential and everything to do with their inability to feel comfortable functioning in groups. When the anxious student is called upon, the cognitive centre of their brain shuts down and they immediately go to the fear centre and either want to flee or freeze. This kind of anxiety often requires professional therapy and support for social comfort to be achievable. Insisting that these students just relax, or just breathe, is not a workable solution unless connected to therapy. A helpful approach for this type of student called Set Students Up for Success is described in the next chapter.

The *restrained (or reserved) introvert* are those students that often make us want to ask, "Where was that performance earlier?" And "Why didn't they just start with that?" The answer is, of course, they couldn't. They just don't start that way. They need to warm up to the situation and ease into things. Allowing these students time and space to do just that, warm up into it, will help them get to where teachers want them to go. For example, many teachers will provide students with an opportunity to redo particular assignments, including presentations. These students may respond better after they realize that the assignment or presentation was not that overwhelming, and they will present a markedly superior outcome on the second attempt.

Evidently, introversion is a multifaceted personality characteristic, and each type can easily be misunderstood if teachers are not aware that this natural personality variable is in play in the classroom. Teacher report card comments about participation in Q&A will not change this. Introverted students will not participate in open class discussions without specific support and interventions.

In summary, the introverted personality type is not ideal for the contemporary classroom where collaborative problem-solving and teamwork are seen as desirable qualities to have and to develop in today's student. But, given appropriate scaffolded support, introverted students can become willing to participate in classroom Q&A when they can see that talking in front of their peers is something that is not going to harm them emotionally, socially, academically, or intellectually.

Given the right set of supports, introverts can be coaxed out of their comfort places, and Q&A—when approached differently—can become a comfort place for them.

Question and Answer Frameworks

A systematic approach to Q&A will support new and experienced teachers in enhancing their instructional impact across all grades and subjects. This approach will help teachers to develop higher-level questions that increase student engagement and participation.

The Q&A process can impact academic trust negatively, as described in the pitfalls section, or it can be an excellent arena for deepening academic trust and expanding strong instructional impact out toward the margins in every classroom. Q&A methods and approaches that reduce student anxiety and build student confidence are required. Let's first examine two frameworks that ensure quality questions are being put to students. Bloom's Revised Taxonomy and Question/Answer-Relationship (QAR) are two frameworks that support teachers in developing their questioning capacity.

Bloom's Revised Taxonomy

Bloom's Revised Taxonomy (Figure 8) provides a framework for ensuring that teacher questions move along the continuum of lower-order thinking skills to higher-order thinking skills.

Figure 8
Bloom's Old and Revised Taxonomy

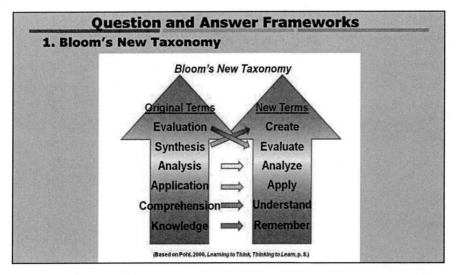

As illustrated, the old taxonomy used nouns to describe the different level, while the new taxonomy uses verbs, implying that you need to be doing something. In addition, synthesis is identified as creation in the new taxonomy, and creation has been placed at the highest level on the continuum, and rightly so. For your convenience, Figure 9 identifies a list of verbs that correlate to Bloom's six levels and are useful for teacher planning in determining the type of questions to ask students and corresponding assignments.

Asking effective questions is an important teacher skill. Moving beyond the lower-level questioning of remember, understand, and apply is obligatory to engage students in the higher levels of analyze, evaluate, and create. To assist in this quest, Figure 10 provides a short list of question stems that teachers can use for developing higher-level questioning techniques. When teachers plan the insertion of these types of questions into their instructional practice, they support deeper student intellectual engagement, which leads to higher student satisfaction and enjoyment of learning.

Figure 9

Bloom's Taxonomy and Corresponding Verbs

Remember Recall facts and basic concepts	Define, Identify, Describe, Recognize, Tell, Explain, Recite, Memorize, Illustrate, Quote, State, Match, Select, Examine, Locate, Enumerate, Record, List, Label
Understand Explain ideas or concepts	Summarize, Interpret, Classify, Compare, Contrast, Infer, Relate, Extract, Paraphrase, Cite, Discuss, Distinguish, Delineate, Extend, Predict, Indicate, Translate, Inquire, Associate, Explore, Convert
Apply Use information in new situations	Solve, Change, Relate, Complete, Use, Sketch, Teach, Articulate, Discover, Transfer, Show, Demonstrate, Involve, Dramatize, Produce, Report, Act, Respond, Administer, Actuate, Prepare, Manipulate
Analyze Draw connections between ideas	Contrast, Connect, Relate, Devise, Correlate, Illustrate, Distill, Conclude, Categorize, Take Apart, Problem-Solve, Differentiate, Deduce, Conclude, Devise, Subdivide, Calculate, Order, Adapt
Evaluate Justify a stand or decision	Criticize, Reframe, Judge, Defend, Appraise, Value, Prioritize, Plan, Grade, Reframe, Revise, Refine, Argue, Support, Evolve, Decide, Re-design
Create Produce new or original work	Modify, Role-Play, Develop, Write, Rewrite, Pivot, Collaborate, Formulate, Invent, Imagine, Design

There will be a substantial difference between teachers who have been purposeful in terms of selection of question types and those who have not in regard to student challenge. However, it would not take long before even the most inexperienced teacher would be able to select the right level of questions for student use from intellectual muscle memory. Practice and deliberate practice lead to this skill set becoming internalized. If it is not yet internalized, continue to work on it, and it will become so.

Question/Answer Relationship (QAR)

Another questioning framework is the Question/Answer Relationship or QAR (Raphael, 1982, 1986). This is a questioning structure that emphasizes that a relationship exists between the question, the text, and the background of the reader. QAR teaches students how to locate information, recognize text structures, and make inferences to read between and beyond the words of the

Figure 10

Question Stems for High-Level Questioning

Remember:	Understand:	Apply:
• Recall facts and basic concepts • Who, what, where, when, how...? • Describe ...	• Explain ideas or concepts • Retell, summarize, in your own words ... • Can you show or demonstrate a similar ...?	• Use information in new situations • How is this an example of that? • How is this related to that? • How is this different from that? • Why is this important, significant, necessary ...?
Analyze:	**Evaluate:**	**Create:**
• Draw connections between ideas • What are the parts or features of ...? • Classify this according to ... • Outline or diagram ... • Compare and contrast this with that ... • What evidence can you provide to support ...?	• Justify a stand or decision • Do you agree or disagree...and why? • What are your thoughts/ideas about...? • What is the most important ... and why? • How would you order these from most important to least? • What set of criteria would apply here...?	• Produce new or original work • What would you infer or predict from ...? • What can you add to ...? • Create or design a new... using ... • What would happen if this was combined with that/those? • What solutions would you suggest for ...?

(Asking Questions: Six Types. Centre for Teaching Excellence, University of Waterloo)

text. In this strategy, students are taught to use four question/answer relation-ships (QARs) to find the information they need to answer the question. The QAR process includes the following six steps.

1. The teacher introduces QAR and explains the four types of question/answer relationships.
2. The teacher models the QAR process by using a short reading passage. First, read the story and questions to the students. Then identify which QARs are evidenced through the questions given. Finally, answer questions and discuss.
3. The teacher practices identifying the QARs with the class.
4. The teacher provides independent practice.
5. The teacher gradually increases the length and complexity of the texts used with QAR.
6. The students continue to use QAR throughout the year, across the curriculum in science, social studies, health, etc.

QAR Descriptors

Questions in a Q&A are about teaching students how to explore the text and make connections between their prior experience and the new materials. Figure 11 offers a quick guide of the four types of questioning. The only lower-level question technique in this framework is the *Right There* question style. The student is directed to find specifically what it is the text says about the question being asked that is located in one place in the text—right there. *Think and Search* requires the student to synthesise two or more pieces located in different locations in the text. The student must be able to sift through the original text and identify the pieces of information required to answer this type of question. The *Author and Me* level of question requires the reader to read either between or beyond the lines the text provides. For example, students will need to be able to make inferences, categorize, defend, reframe, modify, or support their ideas. The final relationship *On My Own* requires the student to draw upon their own experience and make connections to the new text, often synthesizing the material.

Figure 11
Question and Answer Description

IN THE TEXT QUESTIONS:	IN MY HEAD QUESTIONS:
Right There – The answer is in the text and is usually easy to find. The information is found in one place. **Think and Search** – The answer is in the selection, but students need to put together different pieces of information. The answer is found in more than one place.	**Author and Me** – The answer is not explicitly stated in the text. They need to think about what they already know, what the author tells them in the text, and how it fits together. **On My Own** – The answer is not text-based. Students may be able to answer the question without reading the selection by using their own experiences and background knowledge.

The next three charts can assist teachers in the creation of QAR questions. The first tool, in Figure 12, is a set of question stems that target the four types of questions. The second tool, in Figure 13, is another chart that again assists teachers in designing questions that target the specific levels. Lower-order questions are typically the "what, when, who, and where." The higher-order questions tend to be the why or how ones. As the questions move to the bottom right corner of this chart, they move into the higher-level type questions. Figure 14 allows you to select a word in the left-hand column and then select one word from the top row. As you move farther right, the higher the level of the question.

Figure 12

Question Stems A: The Four Types of Questions

IN THE TEXT QUESTIONS	
RIGHT THERE	**THINK AND SEARCH**
What did...? Who did...? How many...? What was...? Who are...? When did...? What does...? What kind...? Who is...? Where is...?	How do you...? What happened to...? How long did...? What happened before...? What happened after...? How would you describe...? What examples...? Where did...? How do you make...? Why does...?
IN MY HEAD QUESTIONS	
AUTHOR AND ME	**ON MY OWN**
Do you agree with...? Why did the main character...? How did they feel when...? Give the reasons why... What do you think...? What if...? What do you think will happen if...? What did the author mean by...?	Have you ever...? What are the reasons that...? If you could...? If you were going to...? What are the pros/cons of...? Do you know anyone who...? How do you feel about...? What do you do when...? What do you already know about...?

Figure 13

Question Stems B: Questions That Target the Levels

What is?	What did?	What can?	What would?	What will?	What might?
Where or when is?	Where or when did?	Where or when can?	Where or when would?	Where or when will?	Where or when might?
Which is?	Which did?	Which can?	Which would?	Which will?	Which might?
Who is?	Who did?	Who can?	Who would?	Who will?	Who might?
Why is?	Why did?	Why can?	Why would?	Why will?	Why might?
How is?	How did?	How can?	How would?	How will?	How might?

Figure 14

Question Stem Template

	Is	Did	Can	Would	Will	Might
Who						
What						
When						
Where						
How						
Why						

8

Supportive Approaches to Questioning

Remember this. Hold on to this. This is the only perfection there is, the perfection of helping others. This is the only thing we can do that has any lasting meaning. This is why we're here. To make each other feel safe.
Andre Agassi

WHILE BLOOM'S TAXONOMY AND QAR PROVIDE CLEAR SUPPORT FOR THE development of effective questions to support student and teacher conversations, how questions are asked also matters. Working from a solid foundation of question development, a few simple strategies are included that support the creation of a classroom culture of academic trust. They are:

- Stick with the Student
- Set Students Up for Success
- Quick Check-Ins, which includes:
  - Mini Whiteboards
  - Red or Green
  - Thumbs Up, Thumbs Down
  - Popsicle Sticks

When these strategies are combined with the question frameworks, teachers and students will find that they are in a much more comfortable learning environment. Academic trust is entirely about how the student perceives the teacher and how the teacher will, or will not, protect the students' sense of self-esteem, self-worth, and competence. Students who find themselves closer to the outer margins of teacher impact benefit most from these approaches. However, all students will appreciate the following strategies.

Stick with the Student

This strategy replaces the Bermuda Triangle of questioning discussed earlier where all participants end up losing. When teachers ask a specific student to put themselves out there to answer a question, teachers need to honour that risk. They do this by sticking with the student that they first called upon to answer the question. In all likelihood, the first student represents other students in the class who may also not know the answer. As the teacher sticks with the first student, they must break the question down by backing up to more basic information until they get a correct answer, and then move forward to the original question, leading the student to the answer. Employing this approach saves face for the student, and all the students learn more about the original question throughout the guided questioning.

A simple example of this approach will help to clarify the process. This scenario takes place in a literature class. The teacher poses the question, "How is Cinderella like a butterfly?" and calls upon a student to answer the question. Notice the level of the question.

T: How is Cinderella like a butterfly? (Trying to link to prior knowledge)

S: I am not sure. I do not know. (Stay with the student)

T: Can you tell me where a butterfly comes from?

S: You mean like from the trees and flowers?

T: No. I mean that before the butterfly became a butterfly, it was a different type of insect. (Leading question to help link prior knowledge)

S: Oh! You mean it was a caterpillar first?

T: Correct. It was a caterpillar first. As it changed into a butterfly, can you remember what that process is called? (Recall prompt)

S: I think so. Was it a metamorphosis?

T: Yes. That is exactly it. Good recall from your science class. So, can you now connect the metamorphosis change of the caterpillar to how the butterfly applies to Cinderella. (Link the two for the student)

S: Yes! I think so. Cinderella started out as a poor, mistreated, stepchild and married the prince and turned into a princess. A metamorphosis, right?

T: Exactly. Good job connecting what you know in science to the Cinderella story. Keep in mind, for future reference, that you will have lots of opportunities to connect ideas from one class or subject to others.

Sticking with the student demonstrates, first, to the student responding to the teacher's question, that the teacher will not leave them out there looking ignorant in front of their peers. Second, the teacher having walked the student through the content, landing them safely with the answer for all the world to see, is perceived as a person that can create a classroom culture of academic trust. Every other student in the class sees this outcome, and more importantly, feels this outcome. Trust is about thinking and feeling, I will not be harmed here. Third, no other student is involved directly in this process. Indirectly, those who knew the answer have that belief confirmed and they feel good about that. Those who didn't know the answer, or those who had it wrong, were all given the correct information from this short but helpful dialogue. Lastly, not involving a second or a third student in the Q&A avoids the possibility for any student feeling like they participated in demonstrating that their classmate was not very smart, or that the other classmate was smarter and therefore superior to the first student. Sticking with the student contributes to the creation of a classroom culture of academic trust like no other practice I know.

Set Students Up for Success

This second strategy works very well with students that are out in the margins and have had several years of negative school experience. Typically, these students are not very motivated and have developed an assortment of coping strategies used to avoid school tasks. Setting students up for success meets these students where they are at. Asking them to perform tasks for which they do not have the prerequisite skill is self-defeating for everyone involved. Skill and challenge levels must be balanced.

The teacher begins with assigning all students to complete the same short task while working individually. They are given a timeline, such as two or three minutes, and they are to put their hand up when they feel they have successfully completed the assignment. As their hand goes up, the teacher circulates around the room and checks to see if their work is correct. If it is, the teacher gives them two thumbs up and then tells the student that they are going to call upon them to share their answer with the class, and not to worry, because their answer is a great one. Rarely does a student object to this because they were just told by the teacher that their answer is great. If the answer is incorrect, clear formative feedback is provided for the student to make a correction. They are told when they have fixed it to let the teacher know so that it can be checked again. When the teacher returns, they give the student the message they have given the other students, that the student will be asked to share their awesome answer with the class. The teacher repeats this process for every student in the class. The teacher is making positive connections with every student, providing each with clear, helpful, formative feedback. When the two or three minutes are up, the teacher then calls upon as many students as possible to share their correct answers and watch as they do so much more willingly. Continue to do this for several weeks and a class of reluctant students will turn the corner and become more willing to answer questions without being as closely prepped as in those first weeks.

This strategy requires the selection of short pieces of work that require students to apply a process that they are learning to do. Make an outline for a very short paragraph, essay, or report. Write a sentence for this topic, or a supporting sentence, or a concluding sentence. Complete a math question showing how you solved for x. The list is inexhaustible and cross curricular. The key is to support the student when it is time to share with the entire class. When the reluctant student knows that their answer is correct, they are much more willing to share with everyone. The climate of academic trust in the class becomes palpable. Meet students where they are at and move them forward with support.

Quick Check-Ins

There are several ways that teachers can check in with their students to determine understanding or to create a lesson hook other than the traditional practice of the teacher asking the entire class to respond to their questions and having students put up their hands with the hope that they are selected to answer. The extrovert vies for teacher favour, while the introvert hopes their unraised hand goes unnoticed. The following strategies are a small sample of how teachers can check in to determine student understanding quickly, efficiently, and with high engagement, including extroverts and introverts.

Mini Whiteboards

Providing every student in the class with a clear plastic page sleeve, or a sheet protector, that has a blank white paper in it creates a mini whiteboard. This mini whiteboard, coupled with any type of erasable marker, becomes an effective method for teachers to ask quick introductory or review questions. Students respond on the mini whiteboard and then hold it up for the teacher to quickly scan the entire group of students to determine how many are hitting the target. If the response is an overwhelming yes or no, or a mix, the teacher then knows to move on, to reteach, or to take a few students aside later and support them further. Reteaching can be done immediately as the teacher models how to arrive at the answer, while all students check their own work and make corrections on their mini whiteboard. A similar question can then be asked, helping the teacher determine if the students are ready to move forward.

The mini whiteboard can be used in a variety of lesson places and has a couple of advantages for its use. As a tool, it can be connected to assessment for learning. The method can be used as a quick check-in, or as students are working on new processes, or as an exit check at the end of a lesson. One advantage of this strategy is that the teacher can quickly determine if they are impacting student learning strongly, moderately, or not at all, and then determine appropriate follow up. This student communication advantage is so timely and supportive of teacher action. Another advantage is that every student can participate by holding their sheet up and direct it toward the teacher with little interference from the other students. Student self-esteem and confidence is supported as students immediately see how well they are doing and make corrections on the go. Finally, student time on task is optimized as there is little opportunity for time off task as each student—working individually—participates and reports their work on a pace set by the teacher. The mini whiteboard is a powerful tool that helps teachers expand their impact and create a class culture of academic trust.

Red or Green

The target audience for this tool is typically younger students, but it can be used by older students, depending on the student-teacher relationship and the level of academic trust in the room. Each student is provided with a disc that is about 8 to 10 centimetres in diameter. One side is coloured red, the other green. A popsicle stick or tongue depressor can be glued to the disc so that when completed it looks like a lollipop. Teachers can check in with the entire class when they ask questions about whether everyone has understood the recently taught concept. If the students believe they have it, they hold up the disc showing green, and if they don't have it, they show red. To ensure that students don't just hold up the green and pretend to understand the concept, there is one caveat— if a student shows green, they are declaring to the teacher that they know the answer and are willing to provide evidence of this understanding. The teacher must require that at least one student per question provides the answer to the rest of the class. If the student struggles with answering the question, then the teacher uses the stick-with-the-student strategy until the student arrives at the answer, and then the class moves on as determined by the evidence gathered by the teacher about overall student understanding.

Thumbs Up, Thumbs Down

This is like the red or green disc tool but is typically used with older students. Instead of using a red or green disc, students indicate whether they understand the concept with a thumbs up, I have it, or a thumbs down, I do not have it. This visual gesture informs the teacher about their instructional impact and they can then determine their next steps. The same student understanding of the answer caveat applies to those who give the thumbs up. They can be asked to give evidence that they understand the concept and the teacher uses the stick-with-the-student strategy if required. The red or green and thumbs up, thumbs down strategies are quick and effective ways to gain an understanding of instructional impact before moving on to new materials.

Popsicle Sticks

This strategy is designed to interrupt the behaviour of requiring students to put their hands up. Traditional Q&A trains students to respond to teacher questions by raising their hands. As discussed previously, there are some issues with this practice. The low-hanging fruit students become the standard business of the class and the extroverts control the classroom discussion while the introverts hope they are ignored. The rule when using the popsicle sticks is that no one can raise their hand when a question is asked. Every student's name is written on a popsicle stick and placed into a can. The teacher asks the class a question and no one knows who will be giving the answer. Consequently, most students will be paying close attention, so engagement is typically high. The teacher draws a popsicle stick with a student name on it from the can and asks that student to answer the question. The student offers their answer and then the teacher places the popsicle stick back into the can, ensuring that this student is still accountable for the remainder of the questioning because they may get drawn again. If the student doesn't know the answer, the teacher uses the stick-with-the-student strategy to help them arrive at the required answer.

Some may find this next recommendation questionable, but it is worth considering. If the teacher knows that the name that is drawn from the can is not really a viable option, considering the current classroom, or the student context, the teacher could report to the classroom a different name than the one pulled. When would a teacher do this? They would do this if—in their estimation—calling on that student without an opportunity to prepare them would do more harm than good, or that current circumstances dictate that they just don't. A chosen student could be suffering from severe social anxiety or experiencing personal trauma from a variety of sources such as: loss of or serious illness of a family member, recent family breakdown, personal illness, or an unfolding personal conflict with classmates to name just a few. Students bring a whole host of traumatic experiences to the classroom and, at times, their very attendance is a small miracle. The teacher uses their professional judgement, which always trumps rules designed for student questioning to create academic trust, engagement and confidence, as well as other educational routines.

These strategies are just a few proven ideas that help to create a classroom culture of academic trust. Undoubtedly, there are a host of other quick check-ins that teachers use to determine the impact of their instruction. Using these strategies protects the marginalized student, while also supporting the strongly impacted student. This, in turn, enables these students to participate in a classroom culture that is inclusive and safe for everyone. Any teacher who implements these approaches to Q&A will quickly see a difference in student engagement.

9

The Impact of Self and Peer Assessment

Learn from the mistakes of others. You can't live
long enough to make them all yourself.
Eleanor Roosevelt

ONE OF THE HIGHEST GOALS PUBLIC EDUCATION HAS SET FOR ITSELF IS TO support its students in becoming independent lifelong learners. While this is an important and worthwhile goal, it is rarely spelled out in each of the separate subject discipline curricula as a clear outcome. For example, the mathematics curriculum doesn't specify, per se, that as students complete the math curriculum that each student will be an independent mathematics learner or a lifelong mathematics learner, and so it goes for each school subject discipline. Generally, this lofty goal is understood and is often identified in many school and district vision, mission, and goal statements. So how do students become independent lifelong learners? The best way that teachers can help prepare students for lifelong learning is to have them practice analyzing their own learning through self and peer assessment. Self and peer assessment shifts students from passive to active learning, demanding that they use the highest cognitive skills available on Bloom's Revised Taxonomy: analyzing, evaluating, and creating. Students involved in critiquing their own and others' work, measuring it against a set of criteria, while comparing it to exemplars of excellent work, is the definition of being an independent lifelong learner. They must become comfortable and confident with making judgements about the quality of their own and others' work, and this happens only if teachers provide the time, tools, and supports for it to happen.

Practice 6: Building Capacity with Self and Peer Assessment

Practice Chart 6 encourages teachers to provide time for students to assess their own and others' work. Peer-to-peer conversations provide real world opportunities for students to discuss selected learning targets in a way that student-to-teacher conversations could never do. Working with peers provides students with an opportunity to use and manipulate the language and ideas that are being learned in a safe environment, and to do so more frequently. Assessment as learning—a metacognitive practice that encourages students to set their own learning goals and assess how they are doing in achieving those goals—is a powerful indicator of real student intellectual engagement. Teachers can participate in many micro-conversations as they circulate around the classroom and listen in on and provide timely input to peer-to-peer discussions. Student on-task talking, is learning.

Practice Chart 6
Self and Peer Assessment

6. SELF AND PEER ASSESSMENT				
Step 1: Rate your current level of self and peer assessment competence. Step 2: What evidence supports your claim? Step 3: What evidence will take you to the next level?				
Students are actively involved in their ASSESSMENT and their PEERS	Unconvincing	Simplistic	Convincing	Compelling
Students assess work—<u>their own and others'</u>—in relation to the criteria and/or by using exemplars (Note: summative grades are assessed by teacher)				
Students coach one another (and themselves) in relation to a learner outcome/learning goal (i.e., can monitor progress)				
Students articulate their progress and set goals for their learning				
Students are requested and able to demonstrate their learning/understanding in a variety of ways				

There are a few simple things that teachers need to consider when it comes to implementing self and peer assessment practice. First, students need to be taught the processes required to self and peer assess. The teacher begins at the beginning and walks students through the process from start to finish, highlighting the advantages of self and peer assessment as they do so. Teachers draw student attention to the metacognitive brain activity taking place and how their own thoughts are supporting what they are learning and that this in itself is a powerful learning activity. Teachers model this kind of metacognition with think alouds—a process of demonstrating how thinking is learning and learning is striving to understand new ideas with clarity. As teachers do this, their students will see that their cognitive struggle is a very normal part of learning. Learning requires the learner to move from unclear thoughts to clear thoughts about the subject being learned. This is accomplished by students talking and thinking their way through the new topic and by teachers providing opportunity for students to do this important work.

Second, the self and peer assessment process must become integral to the completion of the summative assignment. The teacher must include time considerations in their planning of these assignments. Too often, teachers struggle with giving up the amount of time for this kind of in-class work. They feel that direct teaching is much quicker, and it is. However, complex processes and ideas take time as students move from unclear ideas to clarity. There are no shortcuts. None. Every learner moves from cognitive dissonance to clear understanding over a period of time. Providing a supportive environment for this process to unfold where teacher and peer support is available to help move it along is a great use of that time. Students will only learn what they spend their time thinking about.

Third, start small, and move to larger pieces of work after your students have demonstrated that they can manage the process. There is an implementation dip when most new strategies are adopted. Expect this to happen, particularly if you are trying this for the first time. Too frequently, when new strategies are introduced and they are not immediately a smash hit, they are quickly abandoned. The research on self and peer assessment is quite clear—it works. In fact, self and peer assessment is the clearest evidence we can observe that demonstrates our students are moving toward becoming the independent, high-level thinking learners that we seek for them to become. Evaluation is the second highest level of thinking within Bloom's Taxonomy and it is one of the very best ways to use student or classroom time. We need to be supporting our students in making the transition from dependent learners to independent learners to interdependent learners. Interdependence is the highest level of collaborative teamwork any group of people can be involved in, including our teachers. Stephen Covey refers to it as synergistic, in that the whole is greater than the sum of its parts.

Synergy perfectly describes the impact of high-level collaborative teamwork that the adults in schools should be striving for. It also entirely characterizes the concept of flow, where those who are in flow are intrinsically motivated to do the very best that they can and will forfeit food, water, and sleep to continue toward the completion of a task (Csikszentmihalyi, 1990, 1998). And when group flow is experienced, the collaborative team is really on fire. Any such work that students become involved in is the unequaled use of their and their teachers' time. To get there, teachers must be willing to surrender teacher-centred instruction to student-centred learning.

Fourth, keeping the assessment work focused is important. The assessment work must be focused on the specific learning target(s) attached to the assessed assignment. Assessment precision and specificity is an absolute. It is confusing and unfair to students when the instruction piece, with clearly identified learning targets, is not aligned with the assessment piece. Alignment is an instructional and assessment imperative. The learning targets, teacher instruction, student learning activities, and assessment practice all need to be a part of a coherent learning package—a through line.

Planning for Assessment

How do teachers keep assessment focused? Another Covey principle is to begin with the end in mind. Having an instructional and assessment plan clearly in place prior to instruction is an imperative. A clear differentiation of the essential understandings from the important-to-know and the worth-being-familiar-with learning targets needs to be predetermined. Jay Wiggins and Grant McTighe provide a great framework for Understanding by Design (1998, 2005). Google provides a multitude of very useful Understanding by Design templates. Wiggins and McTighe recommend that focusing oral assessments (conferences, interviews, and oral questioning) and performance assessments (open-ended, complex, and authentic) tasks or projects for essential understandings is the way to go (Cooper, 2010). It is interesting to note that at the pinnacle of adult education, the adult student gets to choose the question to be answered, writes up a proposal for how to answer the question, writes an answer to the question, and then orally defends their answer in a doctoral thesis defence. This is at odds with typical classroom practice where multiple-choice questions with a written assignment attached routinely assess essential understandings. A focus on essential learnings encourages teachers to be more selective in the assessment process. Triangulating assessment practice by employing different types (performance, oral, written) of student work is a must. Once these determinations are completed, the assessment plan then comes together.

Teachers who set clear learning targets and foster self and peer assessment practice can utilize these tools for formative assessment work. Is the student addressing the specific learning target(s)? Are they working from the success criteria? Were students involved in determining the success criteria? Involving students in the work of setting the success criteria helps them to become more focused on the learning target. While it is not possible to involve students in this work for every single learning target, involving them in the work of the essential task assignments that determine their largest assessments is powerful student work. Using the success criteria and coupling that information with the use of strong exemplars and an assignment wrapper—a metacognitive student self-reflection exercise that requires them to answer questions about the quality of their work compared to the exemplars—helps to assure the student that they are either on track, or they need to do some self-correction.

Providing an assessment rubric with clearly delineated levels of acceptable quality is another essential tool for student use. Linking success criteria to the rubric provides another layer or scaffolding that supports the student by front loading the learning target and related content of the assignment that will be used for summative assessment. The rubric must include language that is understandable to the student as determined by their age, grade, and level of skill. The Alberta Assessment Consortium provides a great rubric maker (https://aac.ab.ca/materials/rubric-materials/) for those who choose to become members and a wordsmith with excellent examples at this link (https://www.aac.ab.ca/wp-content/uploads/Rubrics/BBRp18-23.pdf). Most postgraduate education masters and doctoral courses have rubrics attached to the summative assignments. It is very clear what is required and what it is worth. Providing students with the same rubric that the teacher is using to summatively assess student work as a tool for self and peer assessment is a robust instructional practice. To enhance this practice, modelling how to apply the rubric and using selected exemplars really gives students great insight and support in how to apply high-level thinking that includes how to apply information in new situations, how to analyze and make connections between ideas, how to evaluate and justify a level of achievement, and how to create, producing new levels of work that they have never accomplished before.

Cooper (2010) addresses the issue of how to assess student work that is submitted incomplete. A bachelor, master's, or doctoral student would never think of handing in a summative assignment incomplete—this would be disastrous. Younger students will continually test teachers to see what they are serious about. Submitting incomplete work is one of those tests. Providing an assignment wrapper, a checklist for completeness, or a clear rubric indicating that all items are to be completed, prior to their work being submitted, are useful tools in helping to resolve this issue. Students can self and peer assess completeness of their work, along with quality, while the teacher assesses only the quality of the completed work. Incomplete work is returned to the student for it to be completed and is an essential requirement, prior to the quality assessment. Peers support one another by indicating to each other that the work is complete only when it is complete. If a piece of the work continues to show up incomplete from several students, the message to the teacher may be that there is an instructional issue that needs to be addressed requiring formative feedback. If it is an isolated student, then that student may need some formative feedback on either understanding the task required, the processes involved to complete the task, or metacognitive strategies that help the student to persevere. Teachers are encouraged to reinforce with their students the idea that self and peer assessment requires from them the highest levels of thinking that they can do and that it is difficult but worthwhile work. The result is that they are developing their own keen application, analytical, evaluative, and creative skills. To reiterate, self and peer assessment allows teachers to provide substantial opportunities for students to use high-level thinking in a supported context.

To conclude, as teachers focus their efforts on the first six teacher practices—directly impacting student learning and engagement in their classroom—they will find themselves on a trajectory of continuous improvement. It is important that teachers do not attempt to improve their practice in all areas simultaneously. One strategy is to select a practice that will create a quick win and then to move to a practice that will require a little more effort. Teachers, as independent lifelong learners, will be able to make strategic professional decisions that will support them in building their professional capital. Who would know better what it is they need to focus on? Be selective, choose an area where you feel you can make some headway and master it. Then select another one and continue developing your capacity. Over the length of a career of a few decades, you will find yourself to be a very successful, expert teacher.

10

Teachers Expanding
Their Influence

*Conformity is the jailer of freedom
and the enemy of growth.*
JF Kennedy

WHILE THE DAYS OF THE ONE-ROOM SCHOOLHOUSE ARE FAR BEHIND US, TOO many teachers still continue to work in isolation for a variety of reasons. These teachers can be found in small rural schools, isolated by geography and numbers, or they can be in large urban schools with hundreds of colleagues all around them. Whatever the reason for the isolation, the research is quite clear that as teachers work together, the influence they can exert is more powerful than anything else they can do to enhance student achievement (Hattie, 2015). Hattie identifies collective teacher efficacy with an effect size of 1.57. It is important to remember that an effect size of 0.4 results in students progressing educationally at the rate of one year's growth in one year's time. If there ever was a remedy in support of all students being successful, collective teacher efficacy would be it. The power that is harnessed by collective teacher efficacy is something that every teacher in every school should be seeking to develop. There are a couple of things that stand in the way of accessing this power. One is what teachers believe about who can learn and who should be in schools, and the other is not knowing how to collectively access the power of teamwork. Chapters 10 and 11 explore these two issues along with the practice of developing collective student efficacy.

Practice 7: Building Capacity in the Belief That All Students Can and Will Learn

This practice explores a teacher's underlying belief about whether all students deserve to be in schools and can be taught. There is something fundamentally different about the way a teacher will approach their job if they believe this statement to be true or not true. For teachers who believe this to be true, there is a willingness to do all that they can to support the learning of every student in their charge. For teachers who do not believe this statement to be true, they will have intellectual reasons as to why this or that student cannot be reached or be successful, thus setting limits on how much they will actually seek to impact a particular student's potential. These teachers will triage their time, efforts, and attention toward those that they believe are more deserving of their time, effort, and attention. Practice Chart 7 draws upon the principles of Universal Design for Learning (UDL) to guide teachers in the analysis of their capacity to support all students.

Practice Chart 7
Belief That All Students Can and Will Learn

7. BELIEF THAT ALL STUDENTS CAN AND WILL LEARN				
Step 1: Rate your current level of belief that all students can and will learn. Step 2: What evidence supports your claim? Step 3: What evidence will take you to the next level?				
BELIEF in learning capacity of all students	Unconvincing	Simplistic	Convincing	Compelling
Teachers provide multiple means of engagement by creating interest, sustaining effort, and teaching self-regulation				
Teachers provide options for student perception of material (audio, visual, sensory), and by using language and symbols, and supporting comprehension by constructing meaning				
Teachers provide options for the demonstration of understanding through the use of performance or digital media, and provide executive function supports through goal setting, strategy support, or other methods.				

The obvious needs to be stated—that not all students are equal—and because of the inclusive nature of today's school systems, differentiation needs to be recognized as a functioning principle of practice, expectation, and realization.

There are two groups of students that challenge the belief that all students can and will learn.

Group 1: Developmental Disabilities

It is rarer to have a student that excels far above their peers than it is to have students that are intellectually incapable of achieving the simplest cognitive learning goals. For example, a high school student with severe lissencephaly, with no recognizable capacity to communicate verbally or nonverbally, wheelchair bound, moved around the school by either an adult or another student, toileted and fed through tubes, and using hand-over-hand supports from his educational assistants to perform any classroom function has very limited individual educational potential. Regardless of this lack of potential, this student was accepted as a member of a class, included in everything that his classmates did, and attended his graduation exercises with his peers. Everyone in the school knew him by name. Over the years, many classmates supported him by including him in their working groups, sitting with him during class or at lunch, and by moving him from one class to another, day after day. There was no way to be able to know if he was ever aware of anything that he was involved in. Did he learn anything? We will never know. Did his peers learn anything? Yes. They learned that they were, for reasons unknown to them, more fortunate than their classmate in almost every way, that they could be kind and giving without that behaviour being reciprocated, that everyone deserves to be treated with dignity and respect, and that life wasn't fair and that each of them played a role in trying to make life better for everyone. And they likely learned more than can be described.

There are many other students with less severe deficiencies who struggle to learn most of what is taught in the regular school curriculum. Many teachers have worked with students with severe disabilities, patiently identifying single-digit numbers and letters even though the student may be in grade 12. The student can be somewhat successful and feel happy as a result. Many of these students can be engaged in playful banter and respond with shouts of glee and happiness as they attempt high fives when passing others in the hallway or while sitting with others in their classroom. It may be that not all students can learn all that we would like them to, but others can learn from them lessons about gratitude, human dignity, caring, giving without expecting anything in return, and just being able to share ourselves with others. Every student can learn, or, at the very least, has something they can teach the rest of us.

The point is that, as a teacher, you either reflect the belief that everyone has the right to belong and that everyone deserves to be included in life's journey at whatever level they are able to participate, or else they don't. We can either believe that everyone deserves the best life possible, whether that be in our homes, in our communities, and our schools, or our non-belief will mean that they don't. If you do already believe these things, will this lead to life and schools being a little more complicated? Yes, it could. But that is okay. If not now, many of us will someday become that complicated person to live with. As a result of an accident, we could be the one who has suffered permanent physical or intellectual damage, or suffered a life-altering medical event, or someday must live with dementia, or suffer from addictive behaviours that forever change our lives. Wouldn't it be great if those who happen to be involved with our care and support were brought up in an inclusive, supportive, environment where everyone was treated with human dignity, respect and care? Or would it be okay for those caring for us to believe that we are a nuisance, too much trouble and work, and less deserving of any of these human-caring attributes?

Group 2: Adverse Childhood Experiences

The other group of students that challenge the belief that all students can and will learn are those that are the red-zone students—the ones whose behaviours can challenge even the most patient teacher (Hierck et al., 2011). Many of these students act out because of the environments in which they live and the experiences that they have had. What is now known as Adverse Childhood Experiences (ACEs)—and the repercussions of these experiences on children and their ability to function and learn in the school environment—is now being explored and better understood. The degree to which a child has been traumatized can be ascertained by completing the ACEs test that focuses on ten life experiences that negatively impact children (https://acestoohigh. com/got-your-ace-score/). ACE scores consider personal life events such as: physical, verbal, and sexual abuse; physical and emotional neglect; and family related life events like a parent who's an addict or alcoholic, a mother who's a victim of domestic violence, a family member in jail, a family member diagnosed with a mental illness, and the disappearance of a parent through divorce, death, or abandonment. The more items checked on this list, the more trauma the child has been exposed to, increasing the negative impact on the child here and now, and later in life. In addition, other traumatic experiences to consider are homelessness, poverty, significant rejection by a parent, foster care involvement, juvenile justice involvement, or serious physical injury or health concerns, all of which unquestionably cause more childhood trauma. Traumatized children have severe challenges with learning and coping with the expectations and routines of school life.

Just how traumatic are these experiences for students? Donna Nakazawa, author of *Childhood Disrupted: How Your Biography Becomes Your Biology and How You Can Heal* (2015), explains, "A person with an ACE Score of four (4) or more is, statistically, 1,220 percent more likely to attempt suicide than someone with an ACE Score of 0." Upon reviewing the ACE test, many teachers would be able to identify several students who would easily meet the standard of four or more. Nakazawa adds:

> Interestingly, recurrent humiliation by a parent caused a slightly more detrimental impact and was marginally correlated to a greater likelihood of adult illness and depression. Simply living with a parent who puts a child down and humiliates the child, or who is alcoholic or depressed, can leave any child with a profoundly hurtful ACE footprint and alter their brain and immunologic functioning for life.

She continues:

> Imagine for a moment that your body receives its stress hormones and chemicals through an IV drip that's turned on high when needed, and when the crisis passes, it's switched off again. Now think of it this way: kids whose brains have undergone epigenetic changes because of early adversity have an inflammation promoting drip of fight-or-flight hormones turned on high every day—and there is no off switch.

Trauma resonates with students throughout their lives. The more severe, the more heightened the fight, flight, or freeze response. Therefore, these students stand out in schools for all the wrong reasons.

The attendance of ACE students is often very irregular, their mood and behaviours are predictably unstable and often unpleasant, and their focus on learning is severely impaired. Historically, these children would be described by many teachers as noncompliant, disengaged, and challenging to work with.

As a result of the behaviours exhibited by these students, school discipline would naturally be demanded by most teachers, the parents of other children, and many of the students' peers. Typically, the outcome for these students would be severe, with the intended discipline goal of teaching them that their behaviours were unacceptable and that there is a consequence attached to their actions. The aim of this approach is to have these students reconsider their behaviour and change their ways. This rarely succeeds, and these students are labelled the archetypical bad kid. They and their outcomes were and are so predictable.

Many of these students act out because of not knowing how to deal with or manage the trauma that they have experienced or are still experiencing. These students are children who need support, not punishment. They have not been taught how to behave in appropriate ways, and it is very possible that they have been taught how not to behave. Nakazawa explains, "Many of them have never felt positive emotions—they have a complete inability to experience positive feelings, and when they do feel something positive, they're immediately flooded with negative emotions." Teaching appropriate behaviours needs to become the major focus of the school so that eventually the school goal can shift to teaching cognitive content and processes.

It is strategically important for the adults in the school to understand that student behaviour is functional. It is not good or bad. The student benefits in some way from their behaviour, therefore they will repeat it. In essence, the student is obtaining or avoiding something, and their choice of behaviour is what makes this happen. Sometimes adults are skeptical because they cannot see the cause for the outburst. Past trauma experienced by the student and what is happening inside the student's head cannot be seen. What the adult sees is the symptoms of the trauma played out in the student's behaviour. Similarly, no one can see the cold or flu bug that can seriously impact the health of a person, but the symptoms are very observable, and the illness is real.

So, can these students learn? The short answer is yes. Collectively, teachers need to become educated about approaches that help students to better cope with the expectations of school routines and, more importantly, ways for teachers to collectively manage these acting out behaviours for what they are. The work of Colvin and Sugai (1988) identified the acting-out cycle and a process to manage this cycle identified as the behaviour intervention plan (BIP). There are seven steps involved in the cycle that when understood can be effectively applied by any caring adult. In addition, Hierck et al. (2011) describe a school system approach referred to as *The Pyramid of Behaviour Interventions: Seven Keys to a Positive Learning Environment*, whose processes are robustly coupled to those of advancing collective teacher efficacy by creating a school management plan in support of these students. These students are most often found in the instructional impact circle at the outer margins where they lack institutional, interpersonal, and academic trust. However, they come to school more likely to get away from being at home in a trauma-induced environment. When teachers recognize the impact of childhood trauma and come to understand that they can have a positive impact on these students emotionally and intellectually, they quickly become great advocates for them. They simply erase any arbitrary lines that they may have previously imagined, and they get to work on helping by applying the acting-out cycle or pyramid of behaviour interventions. The impact on classroom tone and feel is dramatic.

Most often, students who are challenging actually want to be better and do better. They just don't know how unless they are taught a better way. If this teaching doesn't take place in schools, by teachers who are trained to teach better than any other group, who then should teach it—prison guards?

To conclude, all students can learn, and all have something to contribute. The fact of the matter is the bell curve of IQ distributes 50% of the general population above the mean and 50% of the general population below the mean. One half of the population has something to offer and contribute to the other half. Should not schools reflect this reality? Often, a phrase like, "These kids shouldn't be involved in this" or "The real world wouldn't let students get away with that" is used to excuse adult choices and aims to limit what schools should be prepared to do for some of its students. The real world is a complicated place that includes every person.

Today's education system strives to create the kind and caring, inclusive community we all want by developing and supporting the kind of expert capacity building that is needed everywhere else. Two excellent organizations that provide support for teachers in developing their capacity in this practice are the Center for Applied Special Technology (https://www.cast.org/) whose primary focus is UDL, and the Rick Hansen Foundation (https://www.rickhansen.com/) whose primary focus is on creating an accessible and inclusive world for people with disabilities and offers school programs and support.

Foundationally, teacher beliefs about whether all students can learn may limit what teachers are willing to do to help all students in their classrooms to do their best. If teachers can reach the students that are in the margins, they will decisively reach all students more effectively.

Things That All Teachers Have Influence On

Three things that all teachers have influence on are their influence to believe in students, the influence to develop collective student efficacy within their classrooms, and the influence to support and enhance collective teacher efficacy within their school or a teacher community outside of their school, such as in a university class or study group. These three influences are all established by building deep relationships of trust.

To reiterate, Colquitt et al. (2007) found that the three primary determinants of trust—ability, benevolence, and integrity—coupled with the disposition to trust and the emotional response to trust are the major determinants of trust. Ability, benevolence, and integrity significantly determine affective commitment. To tie these components together in terms of their importance:

> Affective commitment is one's desire to be part of a collective or group because of social and emotional bonds, not just for the tangible incentives (Shore, et al., 2006). The trustworthiness triad was so robust that it predicted trust behaviors and bonds even with different trust measures, with a wide range of trustees, and in different kinds of relationships (Borum, p. 15).

It is important to address why it is that teachers do not have control over this component. There is no way for teachers to be able to ensure that the levels of ability, benevolence, and integrity, coupled with the disposition to trust and the emotional response to trust, is present with all their students. In fact, we know that some students are unable to perceive or detect the scope of adult ability, benevolence, or integrity standing before them. Some students' life experiences have erased or seriously impaired their natural disposition to trust or their emotional capacity to trust because of the amount of abuse and resulting trauma that they have been subjected to, or it is simply not in their personal makeup to trust when they first arrive in your classroom. This X factor can alter the amount of influence that any teacher can have to affect collective student efficacy. That said, there are things that each teacher can do—in terms of coming to understand the specifics about their practice and the things they have control over—that will determine how much academic trust and collective student efficacy can be created.

As teachers interact with their students, paying attention to scaffolding their practice for student success and creating consistent, safe, and supportive academic exchanges with each student, that one-on-one trust will translate into a culture of classroom academic trust. Even the most skeptical student can be won over if teacher practice is consistently focused on making all students feel safe, and then capable. Many teachers share comments from their students such as this, "I didn't really like you at first, but you're actually okay." Considering who these students are, being labelled "okay" is a compliment of the highest order. As each student comes to academically trust their teacher, this will directly shape how students will interact with each other within the classroom. As teachers model and teach all students that learning is about not knowing, and that not knowing is what learning is about, student anxiety and concerns about making mistakes are reduced and students become more invested in their learning. Once students are willing to become invested in their own learning, teachers will know they have their students' academic trust. Trust is visceral. You can feel it and so can they.

Practice 8: Building Capacity in Developing Collective Student Efficacy

I have introduced the term collective student efficacy as an extrapolation of collective teacher efficacy research. Self-efficacy research dates back to at least the 1970s by Bandura (1977) and efficacy as it relates to teachers as a group to the 1980s by Anderson et al. (1988). Goddard et al. (2000) examine collective teacher efficacy by providing a definition, a method of measurement, and its impact on student achievement. Further they identify four sources of collective efficacy: mastery experience, vicarious experience, social persuasion, emotional state.

Mastery experiences are important for success in organizations. Success reinforces collective efficacy, while failure undermines it. A strong sense of collective efficacy is connected to overcoming difficult challenges thus strengthening the collective. Vicarious experience supports the collective when stories of how other similar organizations overcame obstacles and achieved success are shared. What a successful organization did to be successful can often be mimicked. Social persuasion, orchestrated through focused professional development workshops that build educator capacity strengthens collective conviction. The more united the group, the more willingly they pursue sound research practice, provided their experience is also seen as successful. Persuasion that leads to success leads to persistence and extra effort by the collective. Organizations, similar to individuals, have an affective state. High-functioning collectives manage organizational obstacles and crises successfully, while low-functioning collectives default to dysfunctional reactions that damage the organization.

Working from these four sources of collective efficacy "teachers analyze what constitutes successful teaching in their school, what barriers or limitations must be overcome, and what resources are available to achieve success" (Goddard et al., 2000). Thus, an analysis of the teaching task and an assessment of teaching competence strongly influence collective teacher efficacy resilience and strength. Working from this framework, classroom teachers can use this research as a filter for working within each of their assigned classrooms and seeing them as a collective, rather than 30 or so individual students sitting in a classroom divorced from their fellow students. For teachers to be able to gain some sense of how strong the student collective is in a particular class, they can review Practice Chart 8 as a good starting place and work from there.

Practice Chart 8
Collective Student Efficacy

8. COLLECTIVE STUDENT EFFICACY				
Step 1: Rate the current level of collective student efficacy in your classroom. Step 2: What evidence supports your claim? Step 3: What evidence will take you to the next level?				
Presence of COLLECTIVE STUDENT EFFICACY	Unconvincing	Simplistic	Convincing	Compelling
Students rely on other students for help				
Students look out for other students				
Students work together to help those who need help				
Students help other students to find solutions to problems				

(Adapted from Band et al., 2019)

11

Collective Teacher Efficacy

You are either supporting the vision
or supporting division.
Saji Ijiyemi

CREATING A CULTURE OF COLLECTIVE TEACHER EFFICACY IS ALSO BUILT ON A foundation of trust. The same drivers of trust—ability, benevolence, and integrity—coupled with the disposition to trust and the emotional response to trust are all essential (Borum, 2010). The following leadership principles are also vital and make sense because collective teacher efficacy is trust driven. School leadership must be perceived by their staff, parents, and students as being capable. School leaders must know how to build relational trust by being interpersonally respectful, having regard for others, being competent, and having personal integrity. They must be able to deal with complex issues by using their expert knowledge and by engaging in *Open to Learning Conversations* and by being willing to implement the *Ladder of Inference* to examine their assumptions (Robinson, 2011). Open to Learning conversations take place when school leadership and teachers have a difference of opinion connected to a work issue that requires a positive relationship to be maintained despite this perceived difference of opinion. Robinson explains that school leadership must be guided by three values, the first being the pursuit of accurate information regarding the issue. The second, that the teachers are viewed as well-intentioned and have valid reasons for their position with the right to make informed choices. And third, that school leaders must value teacher internal commitment to new ideas over external compliance to the new ideas. The Ladder of Inference is a tool that requires those involved in idea exchange to interrupt their assumptions about teaching and learning by:

- reconsidering their selection of information—the data
- reconsidering their description of the data—what am I not seeing
- challenging their interpretation—what other possibilities exist; and
- seeking alternatives to their initial conclusion that they have not yet considered.

Robinson provides frameworks for this work to proceed with success.

Practice 9: Building Capacity in Supporting Collective Teacher Efficacy

It is important to point out that teachers are under the same obligations as their school leaders. They must bring to the table their own foundational trust, their expert knowledge and skill set, and be willing to build their professional capacity to expand their instructional impact. Improvement requires a change in practice; thus, accepting that new ideas can help is imperative. All teachers are school leaders. For every instructional period they are assigned to be in front of a class of students, they are the best adult leader that set of students will get at that time. All teachers need to bring their A game. Teacher cognitive entrenchment is the enemy of teacher capacity building. Teacher transformation is on the other side of comfortable. Practice Chart 9 will help teachers evaluate their current level of participation in supporting collective teacher efficacy.

Practice Chart 9
Collective Teacher Efficacy

9. COLLECTIVE TEACHER EFFICACY				
Step 1: Rate your current level of participation in collective teacher efficacy. Step 2: What evidence supports your claim? Step 3: What evidence will take you to the next level?				
Teachers COLLABORATIVELY build expertise	Unconvincing	Simplistic	Convincing	Compelling
Teachers ask other teachers for help				
Teachers look out for other teachers				
Teachers work together to help those who need help				
Teachers help other teachers to find solutions to problems				

(Adapted from Band et al., 2019)

School leaders and teachers, and all other adults working in the building, are the only ones capable of creating the school climate and culture. If not this set of adults, then who? Very simply, A.W. Jones has explained that "All organizations are perfectly aligned to get the results they get." If we were to rate schools out of 10, with regard to how well they have aligned their organization to impact student learning and engagement, how well would they do as determined by their achievement data and how everyone working in the building feels? School-based survey data can be perplexing. It is typical for school districts to survey the school community, including the parent, student, teacher, and educational assistant populations to determine educational impact. The educators' and the students' answers to the same questions rarely align. The teachers consistently score themselves much higher than their students on how well they are reaching their students and providing an engaging and informative instructional experience. In more than three decades of experience, the author has never seen students score survey data as high or higher than their teachers scored themselves. Never! In fact, the gap has always been significant. What is the story behind this misalignment of the data? Certainly, there is a disconnect between what teachers perceive they are doing in their classrooms and what the students feel they are receiving.

The adults are often surprised about several items in school survey data. When the data is disaggregated for age, sex, grade, race and other demographic details, how certain groups are faring is a revelation. Some of the information can be understood and explained; other pieces are mystifying, while others are just not believable. There is a legal argument in the criminal code that explains that if a victim of violence perceives a threat is real, then the threat is received as real by law enforcement and acted upon accordingly. I believe that this kind of experience applies to teachers and their teaching. Teachers will be able to provide the evidence that this is the time and place and the way they introduced that learning outcome; therefore, it has been taught to their students. Unfortunately, the fact remains that students consistently report that they are not receiving the messages that are sent by their teachers. Are the students lying, every year, consistently? Or are they not receiving it, though their teachers believe that they are? Let us work from two assumptions. One is that the learning outcome is introduced by the teachers, and the second is that some students are not receiving the instruction for a multitude of reasons. No one is lying. Teaching and learning are complex activities.

For the purposes of this discussion, what is important is that there is a disconnect between what is believed to be taking place in classrooms, and what the data reveals. And the point is, there is no real purpose to collecting data and asking students how they think things are going, if the data is going to be ignored, dismissed, or explained away. Otherwise, why ask them to begin with? The fact is that every school—even the best schools—can do better, even if it is just a little bit better. Is there really a ten-out-of-ten school? There are excellent schools, and these schools will often demonstrate that they are striving to continually improve. Collecting data and using it with the goal of school-wide improvement, which can only happen if each adult in the school gets a little bit better at doing what they do, is the only real purpose for collecting the data in the first place. The question must be, how do we get better than we are right now, given the data we have? Doing this work as a professional collaborative team has a synergistic impact that truly energizes all the adults in the school and generates a spirit of creativity in dealing with the complex challenges each school faces. How does a school get there?

The Creation of Core Competencies

I introduce C.K. Prahalad, co-creator of the Core Competence Model, who was named the world's most influential business thinker on the Thinkers50. com list (2018). Why introduce this business thinker in an education book? First and foremost, he was a professor who taught adults for a long time, and second, when we talk about competency-based education, this finds its roots in him. The story goes that his wife once found his entire set of notes for one of his university classes in the garbage. She thought they had ended up there through some accidental event so retrieved them from the garbage to return to him. He explained to her that he was the one who had thrown his papers out. She asked, "Don't you need them for the next time you teach the class?" His response was revealing. "No!" He would make new ones the next time he taught this same class. She asked him why he would not just use the same notes. His response was that his new group of students deserved his very best and newest thinking on the subject. His old notes became obsolete because he refused to become cognitively entrenched. Even as an expert teacher, he was a learner, and improvement was the expectation.

Th concept of core competency has now been used by every economic sector possible, including Google, Apple Inc., medical school training, investment banking, government public service sectors, and so on, and yes, public education systems all over the world. Workforce.com identifies 31 core competencies. The site explains, "We can no longer rely on doing things the way we have always done them or measuring success the way we have always measured it. Applying the right metrics will reveal the path forward." (https://workforce. com/news/31-core-competencies-explained). C.K. Prahalad's contributions to contemporary public education are immeasurable and his influence will continue into the foreseeable future.

Prahalad's last work was entitled, *The Fortune at the Bottom of the Pyramid: Eradicating Poverty Through Profits*. The focus of this work was "to change that familiar image on TV" ... that the typical pictures of poverty mask the fact that the very poor represent resilient entrepreneurs and value-conscious consumers. What is needed is a better approach to help the poor, an approach that involves partnering with them to innovate and achieve sustainable win–win scenarios where the poor are actively engaged and the companies providing products and services to them are profitable. This collaboration between the poor, civil society organizations, governments, and large firms can create the largest and fastest growing markets in the world. Such an approach exists and has gone well past the idea stage as private enterprises, both large and small, have begun to successfully build markets at the bottom of the pyramid (BOP) as a way of eradicating poverty. When Prahalad published this pivotal work in 2004, more than 4 billion people lived at the BOP on less than $5 per day. Things have changed considerably today.

How is this work important for contemporary education? First, it indicates direction. The entire global economy continues to shift and change with implications that are yet to be fully understood or realized. More than half of the entire global population—those in the outer margins—had not previously been seen as a group with economic potential by contemporary business interests until now (2004). The complexity and uncertainty about how to involve most of humanity in receiving a fair share of the globe's resources and wealth will be an interesting story indeed. The one certainty is that the direction is already determined. As such, it is with absolute certainty that we can anticipate that public education will be significantly involved and transformed by this journey. Instead of looking at the bottom of the pyramid, public education needs to continue to re-examine the fortune at the top of intervention pyramids—the red and orange zones—the students that really struggle to make it in public education systems for a variety of reasons. The students that are far removed from the centre of instructional impact have immense potential. As teachers collectively resolve to reach them, and determine how best to serve them, every other student, every school, and every community into the future will also benefit immensely. The multiplier effect of expanding success in every classroom is exponentially staggering. Which brings us to the second point.

A System Approach

No one teacher, working in isolation, can create enough momentum or critical mass to create a fair and equitable public education system for all students. The complexity and size of the work is overwhelming and cannot be done in small pockets of isolation. Educators working collectively with the goal of improving education for all students can tap into the synergistic flow of teamwork. A system approach, more powerful than a focus on self, assures that extraordinary work can be accomplished. This work needs to be purposefully and fully supported from the centre—where the funding is determined—and it needs to be done at the level of every classroom. School variability is the arena where the greatest gap between mediocre and expert teaching practice resides. How can this variability gap be reduced or eliminated?

Williams and Hierck (2015) provide a recipe for success in their book, *Starting a Movement: Building Culture from the Inside Out in Professional Learning Communities.* The power that comes from constructing a professional learning community is clearly and effectively described. If teachers are supported in working in isolation, the teaching variability gap will continue to be an ongoing issue. Shutting the door on the practice of teaching in isolation reveals mediocrity at the individual level. Creating a high-functioning professional learning community (PLC) requires each participating individual to open their practice, making it transparent. It's a matter of simply doing the teamwork of instructional alignment, with the goal of creating an enhanced learning environment for all students. Teachers who are cognitively entrenched cannot remain so, and they will find themselves getting on board and re-engaging in their own capacity building because they are reminded about why they became a teacher in the first place—they loved helping students. Or a small number will realize that they are not really invested in doing this work and are then persuaded to move on to do something that they will find more personally fulfilling. The professional transparency implicit in real PLC work is a compelling catalyst for abandoning teacher cognitive disengagement and narrowing the instructional variability gap. A school staff working through Williams and Hierck's (2015) small text will ensure that this happens, and this is a compelling direction for any school. There are two parts to doing this work.

Figure 15

The Four Stages of Authentic Alignment

Stage	Goal	Questions
Mission **Identifying:** **The Why**	Schools identify their fundamental purpose and develop a guiding mantra.	What do we believe? What do we want to achieve? Why do we go to work each day? Why does our school exist?
Vision **Envisioning:** **The Eye**	Schools envision and create a description of the school they seek to become.	Who are we serving? What school do we seek to become? What do we want for our students once they leave us? What does a day in the life look like at our ideal school? What ideal school would we want for our own children? What are our aspirations for the school? Why will there be a waiting list to attend our school?
Values **Connecting:** **The How**	Schools connect with the moral imperative of their collective commitment to the essential PLC.	How do we create a collaborative culture? What is it that every student needs to learn? How do we know we are effective? How do we respond when students do and do not learn?
Goals **Integrating:** **The Now**	Schools systematically integrate the mission, vision, and collective commitments into existing structures to reach their goals.	How will we organize to collaborate? How will we provide time for collaboration? How will we create a guaranteed, viable curriculum? How will we monitor each student's learning? How do we ensure struggling students receive additional time, and timely diagnostic, directive, and systematic support?

(Adapted from Starting a Movement p. 45)

Creating a Common Vision

The first is the work of getting everyone on the same page. The intent here is to share the highlights of the process that a group of teachers must engage in to become a better school and how this work is transformative collectively and personally. While PLCs have been around for some time, what makes Williams and Hierck (2015) different? Rick DuFour explains:

> A common failing of educators beginning to build a PLC is to jump into the specifics of the process without establishing a solid foundation. *Starting a Movement* not only alerts educators to this process mistake, but also provides powerful tools, processes, and questions that lead to a deeper common understanding of the moral imperative of the work (Williams & Hierck, 2015).

The foundational work is the work of all the adults in the building focusing on and participating in the processes of creating a school that is authentically aligned. Williams and Hierck (2015) explains:

> Authentic alignment helps connect the *what* we do in schools to the *why*. When there's no clear connection between what we do and why we do it, the best a school can hope for is compliance. There may be investment in getting things done, but that doesn't guarantee a shared purpose that serves as a lens for the work, that guides all decisions, actions, commitments, and behaviours (p. 44).

Gaining commitment from those doing the work is the key to successful PLCs, and following the processes outlined in this text generates that commitment as a shared responsibility. The four required stages to create a successful PLC are described in Figure 15.

Your *why* must be central to everything that the school chooses to act on. It is your collective reason for being and the filter through which all school decisions are made. There are so many good things that schools can choose to focus on. Of all the good things, some are good, some better, while others are best. Choose the best as determined by your why.

The why should remain at the forefront while you are:

- Committing to the clear vision of the school you seek to become (examined in the Eye)
- Engaging in the essential work of the PLC (examined in the How)
- Systematically keeping your fundamental purpose at the forefront of all decisions (examined in the Now)
- Engaging in cycles of inquiry (exploring, answering, revisiting, and revising) regarding specific cultural and structural questions:
  - Using storytelling to reinforce and support your purpose and as a vehicle to share breakthroughs to move toward the shared vision
  - Celebrating success connected to your fundamental purpose (pp. 51-52)

Change does not take place overnight. When attempting to change institutional direction, the terms "change" and "challenge" are synonymous. Kotter and Cohen (2002) as described in DuFour (2008) remind us that changing culture is about changing behaviours and this new way of doing business takes place late in the process. When new practices and processes become the way things are done around here, then you will know that the transformation has been successful because it is evident.

Authentic alignment is rooted when:

- As part of the collaborative team, you're either getting better at your job or helping someone else get better.
- There are no excuses, just variables. Your teams focus on what you can control instead of what you can't—outside factors such as issues at home, parental support, socioeconomic challenges, and language.
- You and everyone on your staff understand that every child is your responsibility, and the failure of any one of them is not an option.
- PLCs are not something you do, but something you are. (pp. 53-54)

Unleashing the Power of Professional Learning Communities

The second part of the work of building collective teacher efficacy is unleashing the power of PLCs. The experience of using *Starting a Movement*, and working through the processes outlined therein, can be the most rewarding educational experience a group of teachers ever engage in. Identifying your why and determining the school's mantra all connected to your vision is inspiring work.

One of the most influential exercises is mapping the school's history. This exercise requires the current staff of the school to dig deep into the history of the school, then describe its status, and finally envision its future, moving all toward a vision of a future everyone would like to see. This exercise is extra interesting and valuable if there are staff who attended the school as students. Deep history can be explored, describing key events and people (staff and students), structural changes to the building, and policy changes. This storytelling instills in everyone a sense of historical awareness, connectedness, and pride in the accomplishments of the school over decades. It truly is inspiring, and this authentic experience then feeds into the creation of the school mantra and a compelling vision of what the school could be, with 100% buy-in from every adult in the building. Do not underestimate the impact of the exercises included in working through the four stages of constructing your PLC.

Change is challenging, complex work. Educating your staff about the processes involved in school-wide change is an important step. If everyone is aware of the road ahead, the map allows the journey to be clearly understood and ultimately seen as achievable. There are no surprises then. You can say, "Remember we anticipated this, and using this process is how we work through this issue." A lot of work has been done describing the stages of developing effective collaborative teams that build capacity. We explore these next.

Collaborative Team Stage Development

In 1965, Bruce Tuckman introduced the four stages of team development: Forming, Storming, Norming, and Performing. Tuckman explained the stages were sequential in nature and that earlier stages had to be mastered before the group could move to the next stage to ultimately realize the fourth stage. Later, the fifth stage of Adjourning was added. It's helpful for PLCs to have a prior understanding of the processes that their team building will need to go through so that they do not prematurely abort the process when the going gets tough.

Stage One is called Forming. In this stage, the group needs to determine agreements about how the team will perform its work, interact with each other, and accomplish the team goals. These agreements need to be established early on, be focused on team goals, provide a sense of safety, help to prevent problems that could interfere with the group's success, be reviewed often—especially in the early days of establishing the group—and be revised as needed. Specifically, team agreements determine start and end times for meetings, put the interests of students at the forefront of all discussions and decisions, determine how responsibilities are to be shared, set the rules to ensure the equal participation of all team members, describe how to listen to each other, how to contribute respectfully, and how to resolve conflict in a constructive manner.

All group agreements are kept as promises. If an agreement must be broken, it should be arranged in advance and should not interfere with the group's goals or relationships. A broken agreement needs to be acknowledged, and the breaker needs to take responsibility for the breakdown and recommit to the agreements or renegotiate them if change is required.

Once the group has developed a working rhythm, the agreements should be revisited and revised according to an analysis of what is working well and what could be changed to enhance the work of the group. Establishing group roles such as facilitator, recorder, timekeeper, data checker, calculator, resources manager, researcher, and so forth, and how long and how often they should be rotated is a key component for group functioning. Using recording tools such as Google Docs, Classroom, and Calendar where all meeting records are available for everyone to access, reference, and use to keep track of responsibilities and timelines for assignments is essential. Notifications can be set up for automatic reminders so that everyone is supported in fulfilling their responsibilities to the team and to achieving the team's goals. To conclude this brief introduction to the Forming stage, the worldwide web is available to source out any number of strategies that can be used for generating ideas and managing discussions.

Stage Two is called Storming and is aptly named. Group trust works differently depending on whether the group of professionals are working together for a brief period versus an extended period of time. It is at this stage that PLCs often break down because participants are challenged by their peers to defend their personal positions and to do so in a way that makes sense to all group members. And if some group members cannot handle this kind of open intellectual discussion, the conclusion the group often comes to is that PLCs don't work. "See! We tried it and it didn't work. I can't work with so and so" is often the kind of comment made to justify withdrawal from the team. Collaborative teams that will be working together over an extended period need to go deeper. Often, educators hold personal beliefs about education, teaching, and student learning that are woven into their worldview that have never been clearly articulated to anyone, including themselves. Many educators work at an intuitive level; defending their worldview about how education should be—in a clear, coherent manner—is not something they are often asked to do. To progress from Stage One to Stage Two, each team member must venture into these personal, philosophical, ideological, and emotional discussions, prepared to be challenged and willing to accept that some personal change may be required. This is one important reason that developing your team's why—the reason we are doing this—is imperative. Once we know and agree with our why, the how becomes more doable.

This stage is characterized by competition and conflict. Individuals must reconsider their feelings, ideas, attitudes, and beliefs. Personal egos are exposed at a deeper level when doing this type of work. Fear of exposure, failure, or ignorance in front of peers is a reality for most group members. Subtle, and not so subtle, conflict regarding leadership, protocols, and rules become serious points of contention. Silence and withdrawal from the group or attempted domination of the group can characterize this stage. Therefore, group agreements must be made as promises so that the group can navigate its way through this stage safely. The group needs to move from a testing-and-proving mentality to a problem-solving mentality. Learning to really listen and to hear one another are important characteristics of high-performing teams. The group must also have the end in mind—their ultimate vision for their school. The vision helps everyone to get through this stage to a better place.

Developing relational trust is imperative for successful teams. The professionals need to build relational trust by being interpersonally respectful toward each other, by having personal regard for each other, by being competent, and by being individuals of integrity (Robinson, 2011). The team must clearly identify their performance goals—the things they know they can do—and their learning goals—the things they do not know how to do—and then set realistic targets as determined by their actual capacity. The team must accept that they are working in a very complex environment and that to solve their problems they need to have clear goals, understand the relevant constraints in striving to achieve those goals, and then modify and integrate these constraints to arrive at workable solutions (Robinson, 2011).

The team needs to be able to have Open to Learning conversations. The process is straightforward but challenging. Articulating personal beliefs and being clearly understood is complex work. A person states their point of view and the grounds for that point of view to the team. The team shares their reactions and thoughts and then the speaker paraphrases the team's thoughts and checks to see if a clear understanding is arrived at. The group evaluates and critiques the shared information, then common ground is established, and a group plan is made. Open to Learning conversations is a very useful tool that groups can use to navigate complex ideas and the multiple group understandings of these ideas. It is important that a separation between the person and the ideas discussed are maintained. It is the ideas that are discussed and critiqued, rather than the person who is expressing them.

Storming is a natural stage of developing the collaborative team. Creating a unified team takes a lot of discussion and listening so that everyone comes to understand their actual reality clearly. There is a purposeful, intentional effort to remove false assumptions and ground the team in a shared understanding of their truth. From here the group can move forward in a powerful way.

Stage Three is called Norming. This is where real team progress begins. The collaborative team moves from competition and conflict to cohesion and unification. Having done the hard interpersonal work, the team has become a community-building, problem-solving organization. A growth mindset and a belief that we can do this together has been created through the Storming processes. Leadership issues have been resolved, data is being used with a sense of shared purpose, and interpersonal conflict has been resolved to the point that it will not interfere with the group's goals. There are high levels of relational trust and a high level of academic trust as the team has determined their learning goals together. As data, ideas, feedback, and actions all lead toward solving the institutional concerns of the team, group flow becomes the product. With group flow as the outcome of this PLC work, creativity and intrinsic motivation are very high and felt by the individuals involved in the collaborative work.

Stage Four is called Performing. At this level, the team is truly an interdependent organization. The whole is greater than the sum of its parts. Individual members are high-task and high-people oriented. The level of collaboration is deep, resulting in expert group goal achievement. The group has created an extremely strong identity, moral compass, and loyalty to each other, the work, and the overall vision. At this level of work, the group is involved in genuine problem-solving, arriving at optimal solutions, and superior group development. Group leadership and roles are dynamically adjusted as the task demands. With high trust as the norm, there is high support for risk taking and experimentation. Students in the school know and feel that they are in a dynamic productive student-centred environment, and this high level of collaborative teamwork spills over into the classroom. Visitors to the school can't help but notice the welcoming and inviting environment that they are in. This period of individual and group engagement will be remembered as a landmark educational experience by all involved.

Stage Five is called Adjourning. As it must be, all good things must come to an end. There are several reasons for adjourning to take place. In a school, this would often be precipitated by the movement of key individuals out of the building. Retirement, transfers in and out of the school, and so forth create this consequence. Regardless of the reason, the group comes to an end as relationships and tasks change. The group often recognizes the changes, acknowledges the achievements, and goodbyes are said. Adjourning creates a sense of loss, apprehension, and maybe even a minor crisis as individuals deal with the disruption to their idyllic, professional circumstances. If school leadership changes, maintaining a high level of collaborative teamwork is difficult if not impossible, unless the new leadership recognizes, understands, and desires the same culture and works to achieve it.

Tuckman's Five Stages of Collaborative Team Development (Figure 16) summarizes the development of high-functioning teams.

Committing to the stages of collaborative team development is the most powerful practice a school can engage in to develop collective teacher efficacy and support student learning. It is within the grasp of every school to create powerful collaborative teams by developing PLCs within their own context. For groups to develop through the stages, their purpose, mission, and vision must be clear to all members and be kept front and centre. The team needs to be committed to their why. Rotating the responsibility of group facilitation and leadership is necessary to access team members' diverse skill sets. The ground rules need to be monitored and revised as needed. As the team embarks on this journey, they need to know the map ahead and understand that conflict and conflict resolution is a normal and necessary part of group development. The team must be reminded about the importance of seeking first to understand and then to be understood (Covey, 1989). It is difficult to understand another's point of view if all you are thinking about is your own response to

Figure 16

Tuckman's Five Stages of Collaborative Team Development

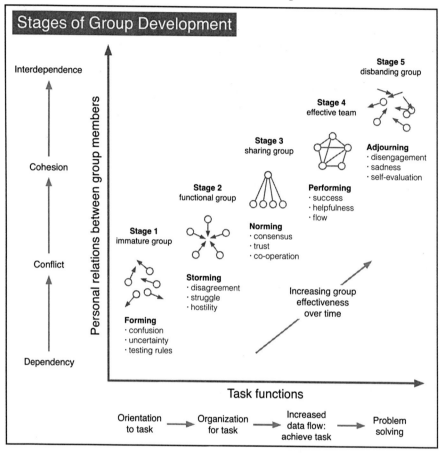

their ideas, prior to them finishing sharing their ideas. Listen to each other. Really listen. In terms of continuity, the team must wrap-up at the end of each session and should include meaningful and constructive comments relative to group processes and actions and record these next steps. Finally, everyone must contribute to the work so that the group really is a team in every sense of the word. For some clarity and fun, included here is a YouTube URL that describes the five stages of powerful PLCs per *The Lord of The Rings: The Fellowship of the Ring*: https://www.youtube.com/watch?v=ysWWGf8VsOg

Chapters 10 and 11 have focused on what teachers have influence on. Hattie explains that about 97% of what teachers do in the classroom has an impact on student learning. On the surface, that sounds powerful. But is it very little impact or very strong impact? There are good, better, and best practices that are used in classrooms, and ensuring that the very best practices are implemented is the responsibility of the professional teacher. If any of us had a choice between choosing a good, better, or best real estate agent, car mechanic, doctor, electrician, or investment broker we would naturally choose someone who has a reputation for using the best practices. We wouldn't choose mediocrity when we know better is available. As such, teacher influences were introduced with the intent of helping all teachers to build enough collective capacity to strongly impact student learning.

Every teacher has influence on supporting student learning and the cooperative atmosphere within the classroom, and they can also work with the teacher collective to expand the influence of the team throughout the school. The skill with which teachers can perform these collective teaching actions is at the root of teacher variability in the classroom and ultimately determines their instructional impact.

When a group of educators work together to determine their why, and authentically align their efforts within an agreed upon format, they can collectively accomplish so much more in the support of learning for all students. Closing the variability gap that exists between teachers is, in large part, an issue that can only be solved by teachers working together to support each other in building their professional capital by paying attention to teacher practice that directly impacts student learning. As Simon Breakspear explains, "If it doesn't work for teachers, it doesn't work." Supporting teachers individually and collectively to become their very best realizes the goal of strongly impacting every student in their charge.

12

Conclusion

Success is a few simple disciplines, practiced every day;
while failure is simply a few errors in
judgement, repeated every day.
John Rohn

Academic Trust: Closing the Achievement Gap offers a balance between research, anecdotal stories, and practical strategies. It provides multiple supports for teachers to expand their instructional impact to intellectually engage more students in their learning by creating academic trust and developing teaching expertise. While academic trust is applied at the individual level between a teacher and a student, utilizing a collaborative team approach will guarantee the best opportunity for any school to develop a powerful teaching and learning culture school wide. Imagine schools where every teacher strives to choose best practices for creating learning environments supportive of the most vulnerable, developing all students into confident, capable, learners.

There is a power in teamwork that cannot be matched at the individual level. Collective teacher efficacy is not an all-or-nothing influence. Schools with weak collective efficacy can benefit a lot from doing the work to become an efficacious professional learning community, while schools with a strong collaborative ethos will benefit from coming to understand how to fine tune the teacher-student trust relationship at the academic level. Even capable young students are vulnerable and would appreciate the supportive approach of academic trust strategies and practices.

Trust is visceral. We think and we feel, often strongly, about who and what we should or should not trust. The antecedents of ability, benevolence, and integrity are used to make individual trust decisions. Despite the complexity of trust, students size up new teachers in about ten seconds using heuristics—shortcuts—to navigate their environment. Trust decisions take place in the brain and how the brain works can be observed. We know there is an automatic system driven by emotion and intuition, and a controlled system driven by logic and reason. These systems work together. Within the brain, this polyvagal system manages at least three neurochemicals—oxytocin, vasopressin, and dopamine—as we wrestle with and make decisions about trust.

Teachers have control over the things that really matter when it comes to student learning. They control how well they have examined the Program of Studies that they are required to teach, and how prepared they are to present the learning goals to their students. They also have control of what takes place in the classroom to support students in their learning. Teachers can build capacity in their professional teaching practices through self-examination and by seeking student feedback about what is and is not working for them, and then adjusting instructional practice for improvement.

More importantly, teachers have control over their willingness and ability to build relationships with their students that enhance academic trust. Supporting students in their growth by using strategies that build confidence in their learning abilities makes all the difference for so many students, particularly those who do not see themselves as very smart—and there are too many of these students in our schools everywhere. Consider the impact of developing academic trust with all students in the light of these words from Agnes Repplier: "It is as impossible to withhold education from a receptive mind as it is to force it upon the unreasoning."

Academic trust is all about how any teacher can help to create receptive minds by competently interacting with their students during classroom instruction. Instructional competence is a lifetime pursuit that is never really finished. On the one hand, it is important that teachers do not bite off more than they can chew, while on the other hand it is just as important that they do not see their professional capacity building as something that is too overwhelming so as to not get started. It is best if every teacher understood and applied Sir David John Brailsford's principle of the aggregation of marginal gains.

In 2003, Brailsford became the British national cycling team's performance coach. At this time, the British team was so awful that a top bike manufacture would not sell them their bikes for fear of being associated with them, thus damaging their reputation. They were that bad. Using his principal of aggregation of marginal gains, Brailsford broke down the cycling process into all of its many component parts and looked for ways to improve in each of these many components by just 1%—marginal gains. By improving in many areas, by a seemingly insignificant amount, the combined improvement resulted in significant gains. These inconsequential improvements moved the British national team from one of the worst bike teams in the world to the pinnacle of the sport just five years later as they dominated the 2008 Olympics. By 2017, the team had won 178 world championships, 66 Olympic and Paralympic gold medals, and five Tour de France victories.

The term "marginal" typically has a negative connotation of being weak or unfavourable. A 1% gain is seen as insignificant, so the perception is that it's not worthwhile. But the math tells a different story. Getting 1% worse, every day for a year will result in a performance rating that declines to almost zero ($0.99365 = 0.03$). On the other hand, a 1% increase every day for a year will result in an increase of almost 38 times better at the end of that year ($1.01365 = 37.78$). When it comes to teacher professional development and competence, the 1% aggregate of marginal gains will turn even a mediocre teacher into an expert teacher long before their career comes to an end. Consciously looking for marginal gains within the six things all teachers have control over, and the three things all teachers can influence, will multiply the academic trust felt by every student in the classroom of the teachers who attempt to do so. Striving to incrementally improve is worth it to everyone involved (Clear, 2018).

Appendix A
The Nine Practice Charts

1. LEARNING TARGETS				
Step 1: Rate your current level of learning target competence. Step 2: What evidence supports your claim? Step 3: What evidence will take you to the next level?				
Clear LEARNING TARGETS **(outcomes/competencies)**	Unconvincing	Simplistic	Convincing	Compelling
Teachers can confidently interpret and prioritize learner outcomes from the program of studies (i.e., can identify enduring understandings, important to know and do, worth being familiar with)				
Students are informed of the learner outcomes				
Students can explain what they are there to learn (i.e., can articulate the learning target)				
Learner targets/outcomes are visible (i.e., stated, shared, shown) throughout the learning process (e.g., plans, assignments, assessment/ evaluation tools, gradebooks, etc.)				
Teachers gather a variety of assessment evidence to measure achievement in relation to the outcomes (i.e., triangulates written, oral, and presentation evidence)				

2. CRITERIA

Step 1: Rate your current level of criteria competence.
Step 2: What evidence supports your claim?
Step 3: What evidence will take you to the next level?

Development of CRITERIA (i.e., what a student has to know and be able to do in order to achieve the outcome)	Unconvincing	Simplistic	Convincing	Compelling
Teachers confidently turn learner outcomes into success criteria				
Students understand the criteria required to meet an outcome				
Criteria is (to some degree) co-developed with students to support the development of their understanding of it				
Criteria for summative assessment is transparent to students (i.e., assessment tool is available from the outset)				

3. EXEMPLARS

Step 1: Rate your current level of exemplar competence.
Step 2: What evidence supports your claim?
Step 3: What evidence will take you to the next level?

Use of EXEMPLARS (i.e., can be a demonstration, conversation, sample product, etc.)	Unconvincing	Simplistic	Convincing	Compelling
Students have access to examples of varied levels of performance in order to compare their own work				
Teachers are confident about when and how in the learning process to scaffold learning with exemplars				
Student-to-student conversations about quality support their learning about high-quality responses				

4. FEEDBACK

Step 1: Rate your current level of feedback competence.
Step 2: What evidence supports your claim?
Step 3: What evidence will take you to the next level?

Provides useful information about performance FEEDBACK in relation to the learner outcomes and criteria (clarity about the task, task processes, and self-regulation)	Unconvincing	Simplistic	Convincing	Compelling
Is descriptive (articulates what is on track and what needs attention)				
Helps guide the next step in learning (i.e., closes the gap)				
Next steps include clarity about the task, clarity about the processes, and clarity about self-regulation strategies				
Is frequent, timely and varied (i.e., both oral and written)				
Comes from peers, teachers, and self				

5. QUESTIONING AND CONVERSATIONS

Step 1: Rate your current level of questioning/conversation competence.
Step 2: What evidence supports your claim?
Step 3: What evidence will take you to the next level?

QUESTIONING and CONVERSATIONS	Unconvincing	Simplistic	Convincing	Compelling
Teachers confidently lead discussions that promote high levels of cognition (critical thinking, problem solving, analysis, evaluation, creation)				
Questioning techniques are used to engage all students—not just a few—in thinking and discussion related to the outcomes				
Summative assessment questions match the level of cognition of the learner outcome they are attempting to measure				
In a typical school day, students are actively and frequently involved in outcome-aligned collaborative work with peers, including providing constructive peer feedback				
Teachers purposefully apply Q&A strategies that are supportive of the disengaged student to build confidence				

6. SELF AND PEER ASSESSMENT

Step 1: Rate your current level of self and peer assessment competence.
Step 2: What evidence supports your claim?
Step 3: What evidence will take you to the next level?

Students are actively involved in their ASSESSMENT and their PEERS	Unconvincing	Simplistic	Convincing	Compelling
Students assess work—their own and others'—in relation to the criteria and/or by using exemplars (Note: summative grades are assessed by teacher)				
Students coach one another (and themselves) in relation to a learner outcome/learning goal (i.e., can monitor progress)				
Students articulate their progress and set goals for their learning				
Students are requested and able to demonstrate their learning/understanding in a variety of ways				

7. BELIEF THAT ALL STUDENTS CAN AND WILL LEARN

Step 1: Rate your current level of belief that all students can and will learn.
Step 2: What evidence supports your claim?
Step 3: What evidence will take you to the next level?

BELIEF in learning capacity of all students	Unconvincing	Simplistic	Convincing	Compelling
Teachers provide multiple means of engagement by creating interest, sustaining effort, and teaching self-regulation				
Teachers provide options for student perception of material (audio, visual, sensory), and by using language and symbols, and supporting comprehension by constructing meaning				
Teachers provide options for the demonstration of understanding through the use of performance or digital media, and provide executive function supports through goal setting, strategy support, or other methods.				

8. COLLECTIVE STUDENT EFFICACY

Step 1: Rate the current level of collective student efficacy in your classroom.
Step 2: What evidence supports your claim?
Step 3: What evidence will take you to the next level?

Presence of COLLECTIVE STUDENT EFFICACY	Unconvincing	Simplistic	Convincing	Compelling
Students rely on other students for help				
Students look out for other students				
Students work together to help those who need help				
Students help other students to find solutions to problems				

9. COLLECTIVE TEACHER EFFICACY

Step 1: Rate your current level of participation in collective teacher efficacy.
Step 2: What evidence supports your claim?
Step 3: What evidence will take you to the next level?

Teachers COLLABORATIVELY build expertise	Unconvincing	Simplistic	Convincing	Compelling
Teachers ask other teachers for help				
Teachers look out for other teachers				
Teachers work together to help those who need help				
Teachers help other teachers to find solutions to problems				

Appendix B
The Assessment for Learning Journey Study

THIS APPENDIX SUMMARIZES A RESEARCH STUDY WHERE FOUR PRINCIPALS worked with eight teachers who had volunteered to collaborate with them in support of building their capacity with regard to the first six practices outlined in this book. The eight teachers represented elementary, junior, and senior high school assignments across a variety of teaching disciplines. Figure 17 illustrates the first two practices (2008 version) to provide a sample of the level of development at the time of the study. The eight teachers were instructed to identify their current capacity in relation to the six teacher practices therein and to provide evidence that supported their self-evaluation. Finally, they were asked to identify any support that would help them move to the next level in response to the challenge to build their capacity. Because the original chart does not separate each descriptor with a horizontal line, the teachers involved in the study holistically determined where they felt they ranked on the scale from *not at all*, to, *to a great extent* for each of the six categories of practice.

All eight teachers worked on the study for a period of six months and then repeated the *Assessment for Learning Journey* chart to outline their perceived development. The principals and teachers collaborated throughout the six-month period, discussing issues, concerns, and progress. Figure 18 shows the data collected from the pre-study and post-study self-assessments.

The left vertical column of Figure 18 contains the six areas of focus of teacher practice, concluding with a TOTAL indicator for the row at the bottom of the chart. The horizontal rows to the right of this row indicate the rating scale from *Not at All*, meaning this level of practice is not done, with the final column to the right representing *To a Great Extent*, meaning teachers feel very competent in using this practice. Within the four-scale rubric columns,

Figure 17

The Assessment for Learning Journey, 2008

Step 1 = Rate the current level of AFL practice (self and/or group) Step 2 = What evidence can you collect to support the current level? Step 3 = What evidence will take me/us to the next level?	Not at All	To a Limited Extent	To Some Extent	To a Great Extent
1.Clear and appropriate <u>LEARNING TARGETS</u> (outcomes) • Teachers can confidently interpret and prioritize learner outcomes from Programs of Studies • Students are informed of the learner outcomes • Students can explain what they are to learn (i.e., can articulate the learning target) • Learner outcomes are visible (i.e., stated, shared, shown) throughout the learning process (e.g., plans, assignments, assessment/evaluation tools, gradebooks, etc.) • Teachers gather a variety of assessment evidence to measure achievement in relation to the outcomes				
2. Development of <u>CRITERIA</u> (i.e., what a student has to know and be able to do in order to achieve the outcome) • Teachers confidently turn learner outcomes into success criteria • Students understand the criteria required to meet an outcome • Criteria is (to some degree) co-developed with students to support the development of their understanding of it • Criteria for summative assessment is transparent to students (i.e., assessment tool is available from the outset)				

Sources: Black & Wiliam Black Box Research (1998; 2004); AAC Refocus (2005); Stiggins (2002); Lissa Steele (Chinook's Edge School Division, 2007); Maureen Parker (Battle River School Division, 2008).

the reported numbers from the pre- and post-study are listed side by side. To illustrate the pre- and post-study columns and how the survey is read, the Assessment Focus item, Clear Learning Targets, will be used to describe this process.

Figure 18

Assessment for Learning Journey Teacher Survey Summary

Assessment for Learning Journey Teacher Survey Summary								
	Not at All		To a Limited Extent		To Some Extent		To a Great Extent	
	Pre-Study	Post-Study	Pre-Study	Post-Study	Pre-Study	Post-Study	Pre-Study	Post-Study
Assessment Focus / Level	1	1	2	2	3	3	4	4
Clear Learning Targets	0	0	3	0	5	5	0	3
Criteria	0	0	4	1	3	5	1	2
Exemplars	0	0	4	0	4	8	0	0
Feedback	0	0	5	1	3	6	0	1
Questioning & Conversations	0	0	1	0	5	4	2	4
Students Actively Involved	0	0	4	3	4	3	0	2
TOTAL	0	0	21	5	24	31	3	12

(Rice, 2016)

Of the eight teachers, no teacher selected, *Not at All*, in the pre- and post-study surveys, indicating that all teachers perceived themselves to be beyond the beginning stage of this practice. Continuing to the right, in the pre-study survey, three of the eight teachers identified themselves to be at the *To a Limited Extent* level. The remaining five teachers perceived themselves to be at the *To Some Extent* level, while none considered themselves to be at the *To a Great Extent* level. In the post-study survey, the teachers shifted with five of the eight teachers now reporting themselves to be at the *To Some Extent* level, while the remaining three identified themselves to be at the *To a Great Extent* level. These numbers demonstrate the movement of the eight teachers in terms of how they perceived their own growth and development over the period of the study. The highlights of the data follow.

As introduced, no teacher reported being at the *Not at All* level of the scale for either survey; therefore, no teacher presented as a beginner in this study. The greatest movement took place at level two, *To a Limited Extent*, as teachers moved to higher levels. The pre-study had 21 teacher checks at this level, representing tentative uncertainty about their confidence and ability to perform these skills, while the post-study had only five checks at this level representing substantial movement from level two to level three with teachers presenting themselves as more confident in their abilities to perform these skills. The largest shifts took place in the areas of Exemplars and Feedback. Four teachers moved out of level two, *To a Limited Extent*, in these two skill areas with only one teacher remaining at this level in the topic of Feedback. The topic of Students Actively Involved demonstrated the least movement. This area of focus began with four teacher checks at level two, and ended with three teacher checks, indicating only one teacher felt more confident and skilled enough to move from this level to a higher one.

The next level that demonstrated significant movement was level four, *To a Great Extent*. The pre-study had three teacher checks at this level, indicating that very few teachers felt they had excellent confidence and skill at this level. The post-study had 12 teacher checks, indicating much more confidence with their skills. The topic with the most change at level four was that of Clear Learning Targets. In the pre-study there were zero teacher checks, while in the post-study there were three checks. The topic areas of Questioning and Observing and Students Actively Involved both increased by two checks. The only topic area that had zero checks was that of Providing Feedback. All eight teachers reported themselves to be at level three in this skill area. From the data presented above, it appears that the practice areas of Questioning and Observing and Clear Learning Targets present themselves as the most skilled areas of development, while the practice of Students Actively Involved appears to be the most challenging skill development area.

This set of data offers insights into how principals and teachers working collaboratively can help to develop teacher capacity in these practices and to do so in a relatively short period of time. This data supports two important findings. First and foremost, as teachers focus on the practices that they have control over in their classrooms they get better at them. Second, as teachers and school leaders collaborate, both build capacity. Collective teacher efficacy is demonstrated. (Rice, 2016)

Acknowledgements

I RETIRED IN JUNE 2018, LEAVING PUBLIC EDUCATION AFTER 34 YEARS OF service. Since retirement, I have literally dreamed about the three schools that I spent my career in, and I often picture in my mind each of the school hallways and classrooms and many of my colleagues and students who worked and learned within them. There were many challenging times over the course of my career—wins and losses, things that shook my confidence and questioned my sanity—but the overwhelming feelings I have now are those of accomplishment and gratitude for the opportunity to work with these educators, students, and school communities.

So, I tip my hat to Gary and Lloyd and all of the administrators, teachers, and support staff that worked at Frontier Collegiate Institute from 1984 to 2001; to Merle, Todd, Stephen, teachers, and support staff that I worked with at Central High Sedgewick Public School from 2001 to 2016, and to Mike, Candice, teachers, and support staff that I worked with at Tofield School from 2016 to 2018.

I have been so impacted by our collective work that I was compelled to put to paper some of the most important lessons about teaching and learning that I absorbed along the way that may help support others who engage in this powerful life-changing experience. And, of course, teaching is always all about the students.

I appreciate that I do not have the skills to convert my writing into a book that others may want to read. My editor, Sheila Cameron, has pushed me to dig deeper and do better with so many pieces of this project, resulting in a much better product. A big thank you to my book designer, Mark Cameron, for his vision of how to take what I put on paper and make it look like a great book and for catching some errors that would have distracted from the content. And to Lisa Borin Miller, my branding consultant, who has helped to define Tony Rice Educational Consulting in ways that I never could, by just asking the right questions.

Finally, I acknowledge the two people who shared the unwavering conviction that I was writing something worth sharing. Tom Hierck was able to see what I envisioned with this topic. Knowing that I was not alone in feeling that this was a worthwhile work kept me going when doubt started to weaken my resolve to carry on. My wife, Tracy, never wavered, and she intuitively seemed to know whenever I needed a push or a boost. Her support in so many ways has made all the difference.

About the Author

Tony Rice, EdD, served as principal and vice principal of schools in east central Alberta from 2001 to 2018, and as a teacher in northern Manitoba from 1984 to 2001. He pursued post-graduate work at The University of Calgary where he obtained a PGD in Teaching English as a Second Language, and he completed a Master of Education for Educational Leadership at Brandon University.

During Tony's early career, he developed the Language Enrichment Program for Indigenous Students at Frontier Collegiate Institute in Manitoba, where the majority of students' first languages were Western/Plains Cree, Northern/Woodlands Cree, and Oji-Cree. Tony presented workshops throughout Manitoba on Language Across the Curriculum at district wide and provincial conferences. He served on numerous committees, served as Division Chair of the Social Studies Teachers Group, developed a North American Geography curriculum guide and exam, and contributed to professional publications such as The Manitoba Teacher, The Manitoba Social Science Teacher, and Teachers of English as a Second Language.

When Tony moved to Alberta to serve as vice principal at Central High Sedgewick Public School, he oversaw the Special Education program for six years and was integral to staff professional development. Upon appointment as principal, he was fortunate to become a member of the newly formed Principals Leadership Academy that undertook groundbreaking work in creating PLCs, managing, analyzing, and applying system and school-based data decision making to school improvement.

Tony enrolled in the University of Calgary's Doctor of Education: Graduate Division of Educational Research: K-12 Leadership Systems program in 2012. This work changed everything about how he understood system and school leadership, systems development, assessment, instructional impact, and student engagement and motivation. In 2015 he successfully defended his thesis, The Impact of Principal Leadership and Teacher Formative Assessment Practices on Student Intellectual Engagement.

Dr. Rice works earnestly to engage high-powered collaborative teams in developing the capacity to align the work of the school with focus on student achievement. He lives in Alberta with his wife and two dogs and near to some of his children and grandchildren.

Selected Bibliography

Anderson, R., Greene, M., & Loewen, P. (1988). Relationships among teachers' and students' thinking skills, sense of efficacy, and student achievement. *Alberta Journal of Educational Research, 34*(2), 148-165.

Band, R., James, E., Culliford, D., Dimitrov, B., Kennedy, A., Rogers, A., & Vassiley, I. (2019). Development of a measure of collective efficacy within personal networks: A complement to self-efficacy in self-management support? *Patient Education and Counseling, 102*(7), 1389-1396. https://doi.org/10.1016/j.pec.2019.02.026

Bandura, A. (1977). Self-efficacy: Toward a unifying theory of behavioral change. *Psychological Review, 84,* 191-215.

Black, P., & Wiliam, D. (1998). Inside the black box: Raising standards through classroom assessment. *Phi Delta Kappan, 80*(2), 139–148.

Black, P. Harrison, C., Lee, C., Marshall, B. & Wiliam, D. (2004). *Assessment for learning: Putting it into practice.* New York: McGraw-Hill.

Blau, P. (1964). *Exchange and Power in Social Life.* Wiley.

Borum, R. (2010). *The Science of Interpersonal Trust.* Scholar Commons. http://scholarcommons.usf.edu/mhlp_facpub/574

Brookhart, S. (2010). *How to Assess Higher-Order Thinking Skills in Your Classroom.* ASCD.

Brualdi, A. (1998). Classroom questions. *ERIC/AE Digest.* Retrieved November 10, 2020, from https://files.eric.ed.gov/fulltext/ED422407.pdf

Bryk, A., Sebring, P., Allensworth, E., Luppescu, S., & Easton, J. (2010). *Organizing schools for improvement.* University of Chicago Press.

Bunker, B., & Lewicki, R. (1995). Trust in relationships: A model of development and decline. In J. Rubin & B. Bunker (Eds.), *The Jossey-Bass management series and The Jossey-Bass conflict resolution series. Conflict, cooperation, and justice: Essays inspired by the work of Morton Deutsch* (pp. 133-173). Jossey-Bass/Wiley.

Butler, E. (1977). Everybody is Ignorant, Only on Different Subjects. *BYU Studies Quarterly, 17*(3), 274-290. https://scholarsarchive.byu.edu/cgi/viewcontent.cgi?article=4126&context=byusq

Carter, C. (2017). The Oxytocin–Vasopressin Pathway in the Context of Love and Fear. *Frontiers in Endocrinology, 8*(356). 10.3389/fendo.2017.00356

Clear, J. (2018). *Atomic habits: An easy and proven way to build good habits and break bad ones.* Penguin Publishing Group.

Colquitt, J., Scott, B., & LePine, J. (2007). Trust, Trustworthiness, and Trust Propensity: A Meta-Analytic Test of Their Unique Relationships with Risk Taking and Job Performance. *Journal of Applied Psychology, 92*(4), 909-927. 10.1037/0021-9010.92.4.909

Colvin, G., & Sugai, G. (1988). Proactive strategies for managing social behavior problems: An instructional approach. *Education and Treatment of Children, 11*, 341-348.

Cooper, D. (2010). *Talk about assessment: High school strategies and tools.* Nelson Education Ltd.

Corwin Press. (2016). *Visible Learning Plus Annual Conference 2016: Mindframes and Maximizers.* Retrieved 10 20, 2020, from https://visible-learning.org/2018/03/collective-teacher-efficacy-hattie/

Cotton, K. (1989). Classroom Questioning. *School Improvement Research Series, Research You Can Use, Close-Up #5*, 1-16. Retrieved 10 December 2020 from https://educationnorthwest.org/sites/default/files/resources/classroom-questioning-508.pdf

Coutinho, S. (2007). The relationship between goals, metacognition, and academic success. *Educate, 7*(1), 39-47. Http://educatejournal.org/index.php/educate/article/viewFile/116/134

Covey, S. (1989). *The 7 habits of highly effective people: Restoring the character ethic.* Simon and Schuster.

Csikszentmihalyi, M. (1990). *Flow: The psychology of optimal experience.* Harper Collins Publishers.

Csikszentmihalyi, M. (1998). *Finding flow: The psychology of engagement with everyday life.* Basic Books.

Dai, D. (Ed.). (2012). *Design research on learning and thinking in educational settings: Enhancing intellectual growth and functioning.* Rutledge.

Deutsch, M. (1960). The effect of motivational orientation upon trust and suspicion. *Human Relations, 13,* 123-139.

De Vignemont, F., & Singer, T. (2006). The empathic brain: how, when and why? *Trends in Cognitive Sciences, 10,* 435-441.

Domes, G., Heinrichs, M., Michel, A., Berger, C., & Herpetz, S. (2007). Oxytocin improves "mind-reading" in humans. *Biological psychiatry, 61,* 731-733.

DuFour, R., DuFour, R., & Eaker, R. (2008). *Revisiting Professional Learning Communities at Work: New insights for improving schools.* Solution Tree Press.

Ericsson, K. (2012). Training history, deliberate practice and elite sports performance: an analysis in response to Tucker and Collins Review - "What makes champions?" *British Journal of Sports Medicine, 47,* 533-535. 10.1136/bjsports-2012-091767

Ericsson, K., & Harwell, K. (2019). Deliberate Practice and Proposed Limits on the Effects of Practice on the Acquisition of Expert Performance: Why the Original Definition Matters and Recommendations for Future Research. *Frontiers in Psychology, 10,* 2396. 10.3389/fpsyg.2019.02396

Ertmer, P., & Newby, T. (1996). The expert learner: strategic, self-regulated, and reflective. *Instructional Science, 24*, 1-24. https://link.springer.com/article/10.1007/BF00156001

Finn, J. (1989, June 1). Withdrawing from school. *Review of Educational Research, 59*(2), 117-142. https://journals.sagepub.com/doi/abs/10.3102/00346543059002117?journalCode=rera

Friesen, S., & Jardine, D. (2010). *21st Century Learning and Learners.* Retrieved 10 14, 2020, from http://tfsfusa.org/files/Docs/TE/Canada%2021st%20cent%20learning.pdf

Frith, C., & Frith, U. (2003). Development and neurophysiology of mentalizing. *Philosophical Transactions of the Royal Society B, 358*, 459-473.

Frith, C., & Frith, U. (2006). How we predict what other people are going to do. *Brain Research, 1079*, 36-46.

Frith, C., & Singer, T. (2008). The role of social cognition in decision making. *Philosophical transactions of the Royal Society of London. Series B, Biological sciences, 363*(1511), 3875-3886.

Gao, Y., & Raine, A. (2009). P3 event-related potential impairments in antisocial and psychopathic individuals: A meta-analysis. *Biological Psychology, 82*(3), 199-210. doi.org/10.1016/j.biopsycho.2009.06.006

Goddard, R., Hoy, W., & Hoy, A. (2000). Collective teacher efficacy: Its meaning, measure, and impact on student achievement. *American Educational Research Journal, 37*(2), 479-507.

Gresalifi, M., Barab, S., & Sommerfeld, A. (2012). *Intelligent action as a shared accomplishment.* (D. Dai, Ed.). Rutledge.

Hall, T., Meyer, A., & Rose, D. (2012). *An introduction to Universal Design for Learning* (K. Harris & S. Graham, Eds.). Guildford Publications, Inc.

Harwayne, S. (1999). *Going Public: Priorities and Practice at The Manhattan New School.* Heinemann.

Hattie, J. (2009). *Visible Learning*. Routledge.

Hattie, J., Clinton, J., Nagle, B., Kelkor, V., Reid, W., & Spence, K. (1998). Evaluating the Paideia Program in Guilford County Schools: First Year Report: 1997-98. *Center for Educational Research and Evaluation*.

Hattie, J. (2015). *What Works Best in Education: The Politics of Collaborative Expertise*, London: Pearson.

Hattie, J., & Timperley, H. (2007). The power of feedback. *Review of educational research*, *77*(1), 88-112.

Heinrichs, M., von Dawans, B., & Domes, G. (2009). Oxytocin, vasopressin, and human social behavior. *Frontiers in Neuroendocrinology*, *30*(4), 548-557. https://doi.org/10.1016/j.yfrne.2009.05.005

Herba, C., Hodgins, S., Blackwood, N., Kumari, V., Naudts, K., & Phillips, M. (2007). The Neurobiology of Psychopathy. In H. Herve & J. Yuille (Eds.), *The psychopath: Theory, research and practice* (pp. 253-283). Mahwah, NJ: Erlbaum.

Hierck, T., Coleman, C., & Weber, C. (2011). *Pyramid of Behaviour Interventions: Seven Keys to a Positive Learning Environment*. Solution Tree Press.

Hoerr, T. (2014). Principal Connection / Authority in an Age of Distrust. *Educational Leadership*, *72*(2), 86-87. http://www.ascd.org/publications/educational-leadership/oct14/vol72/num02/Authority-in-an-Age-of-Distrust.aspx

Iacoboni, M., & Dapretto, M. (2006). The mirror neuron system and the consequences of its dysfunction. *Nature Reviews Neuroscience*, *7*, 942-951.

Jackson, P., Brunet, E., Meltzoff, A., & Decety, J. (2006). Empathy examined through the neural mechanisms involved in imagining how I feel versus how you feel pain. *Neuropsychologia*, *44*, 752-761.

Jacobsen, M., Friesen, S., Daniels, J., & Varnhagen, S. (2012, April 13-17). A Two-Year Case Study of High School Student Engagement and Learning with Technology. *American Educational Research Association*.

Jarvis, T. (2013, July 9). *That's how the light gets in*. BYU Speeches. Retrieved 10 15, 2020, from https://speeches.byu.edu/talks/tyler-j-jarvis/thats-light-gets/

Jones, J., & George, J. (1998). The Experience and Evolution of Trust: Implications for Cooperation and Teamwork. *The Academy of Management Review, 23*(3), 531-546. 10.2307/259293

Kelly, H. (1984). Affect in interpersonal relations. In *Review of Personality and Social Psychology* (Vol. 5, pp. 89-115). Sage.

Kilner, J., Marchant, J., & Firth, C. (2006). Modulation of the mirror system by social relevance. *Social Cognition and Affective Neuroscience, 1*, 143-148.

Kosfeld, M., Heinrichs, M., Zak, P., Fischbacher, U., & Fehr, E. (2005). Oxytocin increases trust in humans. *Nature, 435*, 673-676.

Kotter, J., & Cohen, D. (2002). *The heart of change: Real-life stories of how people change their organizations*. Harvard Business School Press.

Lamm, C., Porges, E., Cacioppo, E., & Decety, J. (2008). Perspective taking is associated with specific facial responses during empathy for pain. *Brain Research, 1227*, 153-161.

Lewicki, R., & Bunker, B. (1996). Developing and maintaining trust in work relationships. In R.

Kramer & T. Tyler (Eds.), *Trust in organizations: Frontiers of theory and research* (pp. 114-139). SAGE Publications, Inc. 10.4135/9781452243610. n7

Lewis, J., & Weigert, A. (1985). Trust as a Social Reality. *Social Forces, 63*(4), 967-985.

Lipton, B. (2011). *The biology of belief: Unleashing the power of consciousness, matter, & miracles*. Hay House.

McAllister, D. (1995). Affect- and cognition-based trust as foundations for interpersonal cooperation in organizations. *Academy of Management Journal, 38*(1), 24-59. 10.2307/256727

McCabe, K., Houser, D., Smith, V., Ryan, L., & Trouard, T. (2001). A Functional Imaging Study of Cooperation in Two-Person Reciprocal Exchange. *Proceedings of the National Academy of Science, 98*, 11832-11835.

McKnight, H., Cummings, L., & Chervany, N. (1998). Initial Trust Formation in New Organizational Relationships. *The Academy of Management Review, 23*(3), 473-490. 10.2307/259290

Meyer, A., & Rose, D. (2005). The future is in the margins: The role of technology and disability in educational reform. In D. Rose, A. Meyer, & C. Hitchcock (Eds.), *The universally designed classroom: Accessible curriculum and digital technologies* (pp. 13-35). Harvard Education Press.

Mohr, K. (1998). Teacher talk: A summary analysis of effective teachers' discourse during primary literacy lessons. *Journal of Classroom Interaction, 33*(2), 16-23.

Morrison, M., Peelen, M., & Downing, P. (2007). The sight of others' pain modulates motor processing in human cingulate cortex. *Cerebral Cortex, 17*, 2214-2222.

Nakazawa, D. (2015). *How your biography becomes your biology, and how you can heal.* Atria Books.

Neumann, I. (2007, April 4). Oxytocin: The Neuropeptide of Love Reveals Some of Its Secrets. *Cell Metabolism, 5*(4), 231-233. https://doi.org/10.1016/j.cmet.2007.03.008

Parsons, T. (1967c). *Sociological Theory and Modern Society.* Free Press.

Parsons, T. (1968d). On the Concept of Value-Commitments. *Sociological Inquiry, 38*, 135-169.

Phillips, M., Drevets, W., Rauch, S., & Lane, R. (2003b). Neurobiology of emotion perception II: implications for major psychiatric disorders. *Biological Psychiatry*, *54*, 515-528.

Phillips, M., Drevets, W., Rauch, S., & Lane, R. (2003a). Neurobiology of emotion perception I: the neural basis of normal emotion perception. *Biological Psychiatry*, *54*, 504-514.

Pohl, M. (2000). *Learning to think, thinking to learn: models and strategies to develop a classroom culture of thinking*. Hawker Brownlow.

Pope, D. (2001). *Doing school: How we are creating a generation of stressed out, materialistic and miseducated students*. Yale University Press.

Popham, J. (2003). *Test Better, Teach Better: The Instructional Role of Assessment*. ASCD.

Porges, S. (2001). The polyvagal theory: phylogenetic substrates of a social nervous system. *International Journal of Psychophysiology*, *42*, 123-146.

Porges, S. (2003). The polyvagal theory: phylogenetic contributions to social behavior. *Physiology & Behavior*, *79*, 503-513.

Porges, S. (2007). The polyvagal perspective. *Biological Psychology*, *74*, 116-143.

Raine, A. (2008). From genes to brain to antisocial behavior. *Current Directions in Psychological Science*, *17*, 323-328.

Raphael, T. (1982). Question-answering strategies for children. *The Reading Teacher*, *36*, 186-191.

Raphael, T. (1986). Teaching question answer relationships, revisited. *The Reading Teacher*, *39*, 516-522, https://www.jstor.org/stable/20199149.

Rashid-Doubell, F., O'Farrell, P., & Fredericks, S. (2018). The use of exemplars and student discussion to improve performance in constructed-response assessments. *International Journal of Medical Education*, *9*, 226-228. 10.5116/ijme.5b77.1bf6

Rempel, J., Holmes, J., & Zanna, M. (1985). Trust in close relationships. *Journal of Personality and Social Psychology, 49*(1), 95-112.

Rice, J. (2016). Unpublished doctoral thesis, *The Impact of Principal Leadership and Teacher Formative Assessment Practices on Student Intellectual Engagement.* University of Calgary. 10.11575/PRISM/28187

Rilling, J., Glenn, A., Jairam, M., Pagnoni, G., Goldsmith, D., Elfenbein, H., & Lilienfeld, S. (2004). Neural correlates of social cooperation and noncooperation as a function of psychopathy. *Biological Psychiatry, 61,* 1260-1271.

Rizzolatti, G., & Craighero, L. (2004). The mirror-neuron system. *Annual Review of Neuroscience, 27,* 169-192.

Robinson, V. (2011). *Student-Centered Leadership.* Jossey-Bass.

Rose, D., & Meyer, A. (2002). *Teaching every student in the digital age: Universal Design for Learning.* ASCD.

Rotter, J. (1980). Interpersonal trust, trustworthiness, and gullibility. *American Psychologist, 35*(1), 1-7. 10.1037/0003-066X.35.1.1

Rotter, J., & Stein, D. (1971). Public Attitudes Toward the Trustworthiness, Competence, and Altruism of Twenty Selected Occupations. *Journal of Applied Social Psychology, 1*(4), 334-343. https://doi.org/10.1111/j.1559-1816.1971.tb00371.x

Rousseau, D., Sitkin, S., Burt, R., & Camerer, C. (1998). Not So Different After All: A Cross-Discipline View of Trust. *Academy of Management Review, 23*(3), 393-404. http://dx.doi.org/10.5465/AMR.1998.926617

Sadler, D. (1989). Formative assessment and the design of instructional systems. *Instructional Science, 18,* 119-144.

Saxe, R., Xiao, D., Kovacs, G., Perrett, D., & Kanwisher, N. (2004). A region of right posterior superior temporal sulcus responds to observed intentional actions. *Neuropsychologia, 42*(11), 1435-1446.

Scott, S., Mcguire, J., & Shaw, S. (2003). Universal design for instruction: A new paradigm for adult instruction in postsecondary education. *Remedial and Special Education, 24*(6), 369-379. https://doi.org/10.1177/074193 25030240060801

Safir, S. (2016). 5 keys to challenging implicit bias. *George Lucas Educational Foundation Edutopia.* *https://www.edutopia.org/blog/keys-to-challenging-implicit-bias-shane-safir*

Shaw, G. (1998). Promoting general metacognitive awareness. *Instructional Science, 26,* 113-125. https://link.springer.com/article/10.1023/A:1003044231033

Stiggins, R. (2002). Assessment Crisis: The Absence of Assessment for Learning. *Phi Delta Kappan, 83*(10), 758-765. https://doi.org/10.1177/003172170208301010

Tuckman, B. (1965). Developmental sequence in small groups. *Psychological Bulletin, 63*(6), 384-399. 10.1037/h0022100.

Wexler, N. (2019). *The Knowledge Gap: The Hidden Cause of America's Broken Education System—And How to Fix It.* Avery.

Wiggins, J., & McTighe, G. (2005). *Understanding by Design.* ASCD.

Wilen, W. (1991). *Questioning skills for teachers. What the research says to the teacher.* (3rd ed.). National Education Association.

Williams, K., & Hierck, T. (2015). *Starting a Movement: Building Culture from the Inside Out in Professional Learning Communities.* Solution Tree Press.

Willms, D., Friesen, S., & Milton, P. (2009). *What did you do in school today? Transforming classrooms through social, academic and intellectual engagement.* Toronto, ON: Canadian Education Association.

Wohlsen, M. (2013). *The Astronomical Math Behind UPS' New Tool to Deliver Packages Faster.* Wired. Retrieved 10 15, 2020, from https://www.wired.com/2013/06/ups-astronomical-math/

Index

Symbols

1% gain, 112

A

Ability, 11, 90
abuse, 86, 90
abuse, sexual, physical, verbal, emotional, 86
academic trust, definition of, 8, 9
Academic Trust Conceptual Framework, 9
Academic Trust Model, 25, 28
ACE footprint, 87
ACE scores, 86
Achievement Gap, 7, 110
acting out, 88
addiction behaviours, 21
Adjourning, 103, 107
Adverse Childhood Experiences, 86
affective-based trust, 12
Affective commitment, 11, 90
affective state, 92
aggregation of marginal gains, 111
anxious introvert, 61
assessment plan, 79, 80
assessment rubric, 80
assignment wrapper, 80, 81
Authentic alignment, 101, 102
Author and Me, 66
autism spectrum disorder, 23
automatic system, 17, 32, 111

B

behaviour intervention plan, 88
benevolence, 11, 28, 90, 94, 110

Bermuda Triangle, 58, 70
biases, 14, 15, 17, 28, 38, 39
BIP, 88
Bloom's Taxonomy, 64, 69, 78
Bottom of the Pyramid, 98
building capacity, 2, 37
Building Capacity, 42, 44, 45, 47, 56, 77, 83, 91, 95

C

Center for Applied Special Technology, 89
circadian rhythms, 20
Circles of Control, Influence, and Concern, 35
classroom culture, 1, 7, 59, 69, 71, 75
Closing the variability gap, 109
cognitive-based trust, 12
cognitive disengagement, 99
cognitive dissonance, 43, 78
cognitive entrenchment, 95
cognitive struggle, 78
coherent learning package, 79
Collaborative Team Development, 107, 108
Collaborative Team Stage Development, 103
collecting data, 97
collective student efficacy, 83, 90, 91, 93, 120
collective teacher efficacy, 37, 83, 89, 90, 91, 92, 94, 95, 102, 107, 121
combinatorial explosion, 30
concept of quality, 44
Confirmatory bias, 15
conflict resolution, 107